193901

FREEDOM IS THE RIGHT TO CHOOSE

Freedom Is the Right to Choose

An Inquiry into the Battle for the American Future

ARCHIBALD MACLEISH

Boston   ·   THE BEACON PRESS   ·   *1951*

Printed in U. S. A.

Contents

Foreword

WE HAVE ALL SEEN the events on the stage and heard the voices. None of us are certain that we recognize the play. These pieces, like much that has been written over the past twenty years, are efforts to find the pattern of the action. Things are being said and done in the world, and not only in other countries but in this Republic also, which have a portentous look and sound. It is by no means certain that we have seen this play before, or that we know how the action ends, or even that the hero is a hero we can name. Some believe the play is Oedipus again — man and his ineluctible destiny; others, the Prodigal Son — man's return, forgiven, to the Father and the Past; others, Samson — man's ultimate commitment and the temple falling; others, Iago — the triumph of the unutterable evil in mankind. There are some too who think the hero may be a hero never seen before: each man, naked, alone, dependent on himself and on his conscience: and that the plot may be his triumph over all the images of fate.

It is difficult to communicate with each other about these things. Men see in this time what they believe is there. When I published, a few years ago, a poem called *Actfive* which attempted to discover the pattern of these confused events, I was bitterly reproached by a young Catholic poet of great intelligence, a friend of many years, who told me it was not possible I had found in our time what I thought I had found. *Pravda* has said the same thing, with passionate contempt, of one of the articles reprinted here. Nevertheless, there is a continuing obligation upon all of us who accept our responsibilities as writers to bear such witness as we can.

To me, as the pieces collected here, I hope, make plain, the time through which we are living is a revolutionary time and the revolution is the revolution of the individual: the revolution not of Marx but of Jefferson: the struggle of the individual man and mind and conscience against the official Truths, the established Dogmas, the organized inevitabilities inherited from the past or newly imposed upon the present. Our time is difficult and dangerous because ours is a time of change in the relation of men to the universe: a time in which men must at last accept the individual responsibilities for choice and for decision which they have concealed from themselves in the past by the acceptance of institutional authority, and which the new institutional authorities of the totalitarian State would deprive them of forever. The future must be won now, for if it is not won now it will be fore-closed by dogma. And the future can be won now only by winning now the revolution of the individual.

What is at stake, not only for us but for the world, is what we in the United States have called the American Proposition. The American Proposition is the proposition that if men are free to think for themselves and to believe as they think and to say as they believe — if men, all men, are free to make their own way by their own means to the truth which is true for them, each one of them — the world in which they live and which together they compose will be a better world: juster, stronger, wiser, more various. It is the most courageous, the most high-hearted of all propositions: the most daring, the most revolutionary of earthly acts of faith. It is, indeed, the one new and wholly revolutionary idea the world we call the modern world has produced, for it affirms the maturity of man as mind and spirit and rests its hopes for the future upon man's will.

The American Proposition was in danger during the war, when the first of these pieces were written, not only because of the fascist attack upon it but because of the ambiguity of our political position, with an authoritarian ally abroad and with powerful and articulate pressure groups at home defending authoritarianism in Franco's Spain. Our failure to define, in terms of that Proposition, the victory we intended to win or the peace we proposed to make was due to these circumstances. The American Proposition was in danger after the war when the doctrine of the inevitable struggle between the United States and the Soviet Union, borrowed from Marxist theology, was propagandized here as orthodox American dogma, and when the related drive for conformity of ideas and beliefs was organized, first in the United States Congress and later among the state legislatures. The worst excesses of the Congressional attacks on citizens whose opinions on Far Eastern policy differed from those of the Congressional majority were made possible by the failure of Americans generally (with the honorable exception of Americans like Henry L. Stimson and Senator Margaret Chase Smith) to defend the American Proposition against its enemies. The American Proposition came under attack again in the so-called Great Debate over MacArthur's removal from command in Korea. The pieces here collected deal with these various aspects of a struggle which is essentially a struggle for the American future — for the future the American revolution of the individual promises.

ARCHIBALD MACLEISH

Conway, Massachusetts

1

Thirteen Candles: One for Every State

Those who think of the Republic . . . as . . . old . . . might . . . reflect upon the fact that the beginnings of the American nation were within the memory of a man whom men still living can remember.

1

THIRTEEN CANDLES: ONE FOR EVERY STATE

THERE ARE VARIOUS WAYS of calculating the age of the Republic. If you calculate it by the steel industry and the present timidity of private enterprise, the Republic is well into middle age. If you calculate it by American foreign policy the Republic is one of the oldest and most conservative of the nations of the world; the defender of the existing order wherever the existing order is under attack. If you calculate it by the apparent belief of certain Congressmen that the American people can only be prevented from deserting their principles by police espionage and courts of inquisition, the Republic is senile.

There is, however, another and more hopeful method of estimating the Republic's age. If you calculate, not by the conduct of its present leaders but by the number of its generations, the Republic is not old but young. Its total age, measured by the overlapping memories of men, is less than two human lifetimes. The Grand Army of the Republic still musters at its annual encampments men who remember the battles of the Civil War because they fought in them. And at the end of the Civil War there were still alive seven and perhaps eight of the veterans of the War of the American Revolution.

We think of the War of the American Revolution as a war fought in school books long ago: a war in which armies and generals move like myths through a distant landscape of wilderness and winter. Actually it was a war fought by men whose last survivors my grandfather saw and talked to in 1864.

My grandfather was a Congregational clergyman of Connecticut named Hillard, a descendant of Elder William Brewster of the Mayflower Company and a man upon whose mind the cares and worries of a war-weary congregation weighed with increasing heaviness as the conflict between the States went on. He was approached, toward the war's end, by a firm of Hartford publishers, who had discovered the possibilities of the camera and wished to preserve the photographs of the "Last Men of the Revolution." It was their proposal that my grandfather should find the surviving veterans and talk to them about that other war, and about the Republic, and about their views of "the present rebellion." My grandfather agreed and the result was a small book of a curious interest, neither literary nor historical but real enough nevertheless. Six of the known survivors were found, but since none was less than a hundred, the eldest being a hundred and five, and since some were very weak, one being actually at the point of death as my grandfather approached his house — "death was dealing with the old man" — not all of them could be asked to talk. Only three were vigorous enough to bring back living moments of that far off time in words which have the sound of the human voice about them.

One was Sam Downing, one hundred and two, who lived in the first framed house in the town of Edinburgh, in New York State, which he had built himself seventy years before. To get to Edinburgh in 1864 you took the Central Railroad to Saratoga, rode a stage twenty miles from Saratoga to Luzerne on the Hudson River and then made your way on horseback up the valley of the Sacandaga twenty-five miles more. The second was Lemuel Cook, one hundred and five, who lived in Clarendon in Orleans County near Rochester. The third was Alexander Milliner, one hundred and four, who lived nearby at Adam's Basin on the Rochester and Niagara Falls.

Sam Downing was the spryest. The day before my grandfather's visit — that day being "one of the hottest of the season, so much so that coming up by stage from Saratoga, we could scarcely endure the journey" — he had walked two miles and a half "over a very tedious road" to the shoemakers, got his boots tapped and walked home again. Lemuel Cook, a man of gigantic frame, had retained the full power of a voice "marvelous for its volume and strength" but his talk was broken and fragmentary. "He recalls the past slowly and with difficulty; but when he has fixed his mind upon it, all seems to come up clear." How firmly he was able to fix his mind upon it my grandfather makes evident: "He has voted the Democratic ticket since the organization of the government, supposing that it still represents the same party that it did in Jefferson's time."

But if Sam Downing could walk five miles on the hottest day of a hot summer, and if Lemuel Cook, with his great voice and his stubborn loyalty to the past, could feel his way back through the difficult words to the actual bloody business of soldiering and war, it was little Alexander Milliner, the ancient drummer boy, who was the real miracle. Alexander Milliner had had nine children, forty-three grandchildren, seventeen great-grandchildren, and three great-great-grandchildren, but nevertheless "for sixty-two years he and his wife had lived together without a death in the family or a coffin in the house." He had never troubled himself about his health — "he uses tea and coffee and still takes regularly his dram" — could read his Bible without glasses at a hundred and four, played his drums "with excellent time and flour-

ishes" and sang songs "both amorous and warlike . . . half a
dozen verses successively, giving correctly both the words
and the tune." Only when it came to long connected accounts
of the war did Alexander Milliner's memory fail him and
even there he proved to be able to recall precisely individual
events which had happened as much as ninety years before.

Samuel Downing, whom my grandfather found beside his
framed house at the end of the narrow valley of the Sacandaga
at noon of a summer day, "seated between two bee-hives,
bending over, leaning upon his cane and looking on the
ground, an old man . . .," was ready enough to talk about
the bees ("they don't hurt me and I don't hurt them"), the
weather ("if I had my way about it, I should like it about so;
but we can't do that: we have to take it as it comes"), and
the war.

"What do you think (General Washington) would say if
he was here now?"

"Say! I don't know. But he'd be mad to see me sitting
here. I tell 'em if they'll give me a horse I'll go as it is. If
the rebels come here I shall sartingly take my gun. I can see
best furtherest off."

"You don't believe, then, in letting men stay at their
homes and help the enemy?"

"Not by a grand sight!" And then, lost in the other war:
"The men that caught André were true. He wanted to get
away, offered them everything. Washington hated to hang
him; he cried they said."

Whether or not the old man understood what lay behind
my grandfather's question — the whole misery of the draft
in the last months of the Civil War — he understood the
nature of the problem of loyalty and the minds of the two met
at a point in the history of their country which was not very
far away to either of them.

Sam Downing's story of his enlistment in the Continental Army went back to his childhood in Newburyport in the Commonwealth of Massachusetts. There, in the absence of his parents over the Bay, a man had carried him off as an apprentice to learn the trade of spinning-wheel making in the town of Antrim out past Haverhill. "It was the fall of the year. I remember the fruit was on the ground, and I went out and gathered it. I was happy yet." But six years later the happiness had worn off and he ran away to enlist, making his way to Colonel Fifield over in Charleston who accepted him, small as he was, but wasn't quite ready to go: "He had his haying to do; so I stayed with him and helped him through it and then I started for the war." He remembered guarding wagons from Exeter to Springfield, and the fighting in the Mohawk Valley and General Arnold and General Gates.

"Arnold was our fighting general, and a bloody fellow he was. He didn't care for nothing; he'd ride right in. It was 'Come on, boys!' twasn't 'Go, boys!.' He was as brave a man as ever lived. He was dark skinned, with black hair, of middling height. There wasn't any waste timber in him. He was a stern looking man but kind to his soldiers. They didn't treat him right: he ought to have had Burgoyne's sword. But he ought to have been true.

"Gates was an old granny looking fellow. When Burgoyne came up to surrender his sword, he said to Gates, 'Are you a general? You look more like a granny than you do a general.' 'I be a granny,' said Gates, 'and I've delivered you of ten thousand men today.' "

Sam Downing had taken part in the later campaigns around New York. "There's always policy, you know, in war. We made the British think we were coming to take the city. We drew up in line of battle: the British drew up over there." He pointed over the bee-hives. "They looked very handsome.

But Washington went south to Yorktown. Lafayette laid down the white sticks, and we threw up entrenchments by them. We were right opposite Washington's headquarters."

Was Washington as fine looking a man as he was reported, my grandfather wanted to know. "Oh!" said the old man, lifting up both hands and pausing. "But you never got a smile out of him. He was a nice man. We loved him. They'd sell their lives for him."

That was the end of the Revolution for Sam Downing, but not of the talk beside the bee-hives. There had been other wars before and after. Sam Downing's father and his wife's father had been out in the French War. His grandson had fought in "the present rebellion" from the beginning. They talked of both but in the end the old man came back to the War of Independence. "When peace was declared we burnt thirteen candles in every hut, one for each State." A man who will think back can see those candles from here in the oiled windows under the tremendous trees.

Alexander Milliner had seen even more of his country's battles. He had been born at Quebec, the son of an artificer in Wolfe's army who died on the Heights of Abraham ("at the close of the battle, lying down to drink at a spring on the plain . . .") and an English woman whom her son described as "high larnt." British-bred though he was, however, Alexander Milliner had served six and a half years in the American Army in the Revolution, five and a half years in the American Navy in and through the War of 1812 — three of them on the frigate Constitution — uncounted months in the Indian Wars in the Mohawk Valley. He had seen action at White Plains — "a nasty battle" — the Brandywine, Saratoga, Monmouth, Yorktown, the Indian attack on Fort Stanwix. He had been in the fight between the Constitution and the British ships Cyane and Levant. He had been badly wounded at

Monmouth and captured at sea by the French who mistreated him in prison at Guadeloupe, feeding him bread worse than he had eaten "in seven kingdoms."

Only the brightest moments came back clear — Washington first and clearest. He had served for four years in Washington's Life Guard as drummer boy, his mother following along as washer-woman to be near her son. Washington was "a good man, a beautiful man. He was always pleasant, never changed countenance but wore the same in defeat and retreat as in victory." "Lady Washington . . . was a short thick woman; very pleasant and kind." "They took a great notion to me. One day the General sent for me to come up to headquarters . . . The Life Guard came out and paraded and the roll was called. There was an Englishman, Bill Dorchester; the General said to him, 'Come, Bill, play up this 'ere Yorkshire tune.' When he got through, the General told me to play. So I took the drum, overhauled her, braced her up, and played a tune. The General put his hand in his pocket and gave me three dollars . . ."

At Valley Forge, "Lady Washington visited the army. She used thorns instead of pins on her clothes. The poor soldiers had bloody feet." And then back to the General. "We were going along one day, slow march, and came to where the boys were jerking stones. 'Halt!' came the command. 'Now, boys,' said the General, 'I will show you how to jerk a stone.' He beat 'em all. He smiled but didn't laugh out." (In my grandfather's copy of his book a letter has been placed between the leaves at this point. It is dated at Boston the 15 January, 1865, and signed by Edward Everett. "The Biographies," says Mr. Everett with that restraint which was expected of great men and Bostonians, "appear to contain all that can be expected." The anecdote of General Washington stopping to jerk stones with his men, he continues, is excellent and is "in accordance with the traditions of his Youth which describe him as being able to throw a stone across the Rappahannock below Fredericksburg." Mr. Milliner would doubtless have been grateful for this endorsement.)

Of Arnold, Alexander Milliner's opinion was much like Sam Downing's. "Arnold was a smart man; they didn't serve him quite straight." Cornwallis was "a fine looking man; very mild." The drummer boy shook hands with him at Yorktown. "The day after the surrender the Life Guard came up. Cornwallis sat on an old bench. 'Halt!' he ordered; then looked at us — viewed us." General Lee was a large man. "He had a most enormous nose. One day a man met him and turned his nose away. 'What do you do that for, you damned rascal?' says he."

The Indian fighting was farther away in the old man's mind and more nearly forgotten. Only the attack on Fort Stanwix remained and that in a kind of broken etching of sharp and dreadful lines. "The Indians burnt all before them. Our women came down in their shirt tails. The Indians got one of our young ones, stuck pine splinters into it and set them afire. They came down a good body of 'em. We had a smart engagement with 'em and whipped 'em. One of 'em got up into a tree — a sharp shooter. He killed our men when they went after water. The colonel see where he was, and says, 'Draw up the twenty-four pounder and load it with grape, canister and ball.' They did it. The Indian sat up in a crotch of the tree. They fired and shot the top of the tree off. The Indian gave a leap and a yell and came down. Three brigades got there just in the nick of time. The Massachusetts Grenadiers and the Connecticut troops went forward and the Indians fled."

When the Civil War broke out the old man had wanted to take his drum and go down to Rochester and "beat for

volunteers." It would have been a sight to remember —
Washington's drummer boy, no bigger than a boy still for all
his thatch of white hair, beating his revolutionary drum for
volunteers to save the Union because it was "too bad this
country, so hardly got, should be destroyed by its own
people." They hadn't let him go, but just before my grandfather's visit he had marched to the church on his one hundred
and fourth birthday at the head of a procession of Pioneers
of Monroe County, where, after they had sung Washington's
Funeral Hymn and heard a memorial address, he had stood
on a seat where all could see him and thanked them for their
kind attention and appealed to them all to be true to their
country, adding with a wry, but not wholly irrelevant, emphasis
that he had seen worse looking visages than his own hung up
by the neck.

Lemuel Cook, with his great frame and his voice marvelous
for its volume, was the oldest of the survivors, having been
born in Litchfield County in Connecticut almost a hundred
and five years before. He had served through the entire war,
being mustered in at the age of sixteen "at Northampton in
the Bay State, Second Regiment, Light Dragoons; Sheldon,
Colonel; Stanton, Captain"; mustered out at Danbury, Connecticut, at the age of twenty-four. He had been in the bitter
fighting in Westchester County and the battle of the Brandywine and he had seen Cornwallis's surrender. But what gives
his recollection, in my grandfather's report of it, so moving
a character is not the importance of the events the old man
relates but the character of the images which return to his
mind. Recalling the past painfully as though from a great
distance, and speaking with a very imperfect articulation "so
that it is with difficulty that his story can be made out," Lemuel
Cook nevertheless conveys a sense of actuality which neither of
the others gives. His fragmentary recollections, recovered

from far back beneath the years of his life before his fight with the Indian in the public house in Utica, before his marriage with Hannah Curtis in Cheshire, have the authenticity of an arrow head or a uniform button found in a clearing where a wall once was.

"In conversation with him," my grandfather wrote, "he has to be left to the course of his own thoughts, inquiries and suggestions appearing to confuse him." The course of the old man's thoughts took him from his first whiff of gunpowder at Valentine's Hill in Westchester County ("Up came Darrow, good old soul! . . . said 'Lem, what do you think of gunpowder? Smell good to you?' ") to the first time he was fired at personally and in earnest (" 'Lem, they mean you; go on the other side of the road' ") to his first sight of the French in action ("They stepped as though on edge. They were a dreadful proud nation") to the siege and surrender at Yorktown.

"Baron Steuben was muster master. He had us called out to select men and horses fit for service. When he came to me he said, 'Young man, how old are you?' I told him. 'Be on the ground tomorrow morning at nine o'clock,' said he. My colonel didn't like to have me go . . . 'You're a fool,' said the rest, 'they're going to storm New York.' No more idea of it than of going to Flanders. My horse was a bay and pretty. . . . We marched off toward White Plains. Then 'left wheel' and struck right north. Got to King's Ferry below Tarrytown. There were boats, scows. We went right across into the Jerseys. That night I stood with my back to a tree.

"Then we went on to the head of Elk.

"There the French were. It was dusty; 'peared to me I should have choked to death. One of 'em handed me his canteen. 'Lem,' said he, 'take a good horn — we're going to march all night.' I didn't know what it was so I took a full drink. It liked to have strangled me.

"Then we were in Virginia. There wasn't much fighting. Old Rochambeau told 'em, 'I'll land five hundred from the fleet against your eight hundred.' But they darsn't.

"We were on a kind of side hill. We had plaguey little to eat and nothing to drink under Heaven. We hove up some brush to keep the flies off.

"Washington ordered that there should be no laughing at the British; said it was bad enough to have to surrender without being insulted. The army came out with guns clubbed on their backs. They were paraded on a great smooth lot, and there they stacked their arms. Then came the devil — old women, and all. One said, 'I wonder if the damned Yankees will give me any bread.'

"The horses were starved out. Washington turned out with his horses and helped 'em up the hill. When they see the artillery, they said, 'There, them's the very artillery that belonged to Burgoyne.'

"Greene come from the southward: the awfullest set you ever see. Some, I should presume, had a pint of lice on 'em. No boots or shoes . . ."

Lem Cook and my grandfather are both dead — Lem Cook a few days after they talked — but the words have breath in them still. They bring the War of the American Revolution out of a scholar's past and put it down where it belongs, within the hearing of living ears. Those who think of the Republic which that war created as already old — those who think of the Declaration on which it was fought as a declaration of antiquated principles which must now be surrendered to the authority of a party or a church — those who doubt and are timid and afraid — might do worse than to reflect upon the fact that the beginnings of the American nation were within the memory of a man whom men still living can remember. They might do worse, too, than recall to mind Sam Downing's thirteen candles and the hope they stood for. That hope has not gone out.

1948

2

The Unimagined America

We have the power and the courage and the resources of experience to create a nation such as men have never seen. And, more than that, we have the moment of creation in our hands.

2

THE UNIMAGINED AMERICA

THE PROPOSITION CAN BE PUT AS FOLLOWS: that the American future is in issue in our time as it has been in issue only twice before; that in so far as the determination of the American future depends upon the American people, it depends upon their power to imagine such a future as they want and can believe in; that they have not imagined such a future, but seem rather to be unable or unwilling to consider what they wish their lives to be; that this failure of imagination will affect our victory in this war and may, indeed, lose us our victory.

I think it will not be questioned that the American future is in issue. There are some, I know, who do not wish to think so. There are some who would like to suppress the future for the duration of the war and to forbid the people to discuss it. They are noisy but not numerous. The great majority of the American people understand very well that this war is not a war only, but an end and a beginning — an end to things known and a beginning of things unknown. We have smelled the wind in the streets that changes weather. We know that whatever the world will be when the war ends, the world will be different.

There is hardly a meeting of three men in earnestness that does not say so. The talk about war aims, about peace aims, about post-war plans, is talk, at bottom, about nothing else but this. It is not the formal negotiation of a treaty of peace which concerns us, but the human negotiation of our personal lives: not the determination of the frontiers or the ratification of the international agreements, but the actual and present world that men will live in when the war ends.

It will not be too seriously questioned either, I believe, that the determination of the American future in this time of change depends, in so far as it depends upon ourselves, upon our power to imagine such a future as we can believe in. There is, it is true, a theory that the future of any society depends very little on the purposes of men themselves — that their systems of industry and economics determine what they must become.

That theory has not appealed to Americans. We remember that a hundred and sixty-seven years ago, at another moment of decision in our history, our predecessors did imagine such a future as they could believe in, and that the image they conceived had consequences. We remember also that after another war, a war that many living men took part in, we left the future to the laws of economics to construct. And we recall that future: it is now our past. We recall a future that should have been peace and freedom and became the radio, the automobile, and the depression of 1929.

There may be some who would like to repeat that future with cheap planes in the place of the automobile, and plastics succeeding refrigerators. There may be some, but not many. Most of us have learned the lesson once for all. Most of us know now that you do not fight a war for the privilege of buying things and then not buying them — for the privilege of becoming the world's most numerous consumers and thereafter the world's most numerous unemployed. Most of us know now that if you leave your future to the markets and the manufacturers to plan, you will get the future that the markets and the manufacturers can think of. And we know that future. Planes instead of cars, plastics instead of radios — we know it all. We know it and have lived it, and we don't propose, I think, to live it through again.

Nevertheless — and this is the strange and contradictory heart of our dilemma — nevertheless, we are apparently not willing to propose our future for ourselves. We are unwilling or we are unable to commit the act of the imagination for ourselves — to say for ourselves what we mean our lives to be. We know, if we know anything, that the disaster of 1929 was a failure not of wealth but of will, and not of will so much as of the purpose of the will. Starvation in the midst of plenty is not a paradox. It is a declaration of moral and intellectual bankruptcy. For if the means to cure the ill exist and are not used, the failure is a failure of decision, an inability to choose. And yet, in all our present talk of change, there is no talk of choice, no talk of affirmative purpose — none, to be blunt, of a people's dream of its future, a people's vision of the future it proposes to create.

There is, it is true, a deep, unreasoning conviction in the minds of people here, as in the minds of people elsewhere, that this war, whatever was true of wars before, *must* have consequences — that anything that costs in life and suffering what this war is costing *must* purchase, not merely an end to itself, but something else, something admirable, something of human worth and human significance. It is a profoundly held conviction and one that neither the superior wisdom of wise men nor the cheapening cynicism of cynical men can dispose of. Those indeed who try to silence that conviction, or to laugh it off, or trick it, will end certainly where the cynical and the wise who fool with the terrible sincerity of the people have always ended. The people of the world *believe* that all the anguish of this generation cannot go for nothing. They

believe it in spite of the lessons of history. They believe it in
spite of the last war and the war before that and the war before
that one.

But their belief is the passive belief of powerful hope, not
the active belief of determined purpose. All our talk is of
the world we should avoid and of the ways we should avoid
it — how to police our enemies, how to disarm the aggressors,
how to avoid unemployment, how to escape the errors of the
peace we made before. At the worst we talk like fortune-
tellers of the dangers we foresee. At the best we talk like
lawyers of devices — ways and means.

We debate bitterly whether business should do it or government should do it, but what it is that government should do
or that private business should do, we do not even ask. We
argue whether to do it by air, and, if so, on what conditions;
we consider the question whether to do it at home or to do it
abroad, but what we propose to do by the use of the air
or at home or wherever, we have not said — what we propose
to do in terms of men, of men's lives, of human realities.
Never at any point or by any mouth have we talked as a virile
and creative people talks in its moments of decision — as men,
for example, talked in Philadelphia in a certain summer when
they pledged their sacred honor, and their lives.

Our silence on these things, moreover, is not merely silence.
We are not all of us mute and dumb. We have words to say.
But the words are contemptuous words. We are shamefaced
and self-conscious when we hear the talk of purposes — of our
purpose as a nation, of our purpose to construct the greatness
of this nation. The word itself and the whole conception of
"planning" distress us. We think of ourselves — some of us
anyway think of ourselves — as a practical, hard-headed
people who aren't taken in by utopias, who can't be fooled
by the talk about better worlds, who know too much for talk

like that — a people famous for salt, ironical, practical, hard good-sense who can't be bamboozled with talk about dreams and visions.

It is a strange and curious picture of Americans. If ever a people had behind them a tradition of great purposes, tremendous dreams, the people of America have that tradition. There is not one of us, there is not a child in this Republic, who does not know the story. The whole history of our continent is a history of the imagination. Men imagined land beyond the sea and found it. Men imagined the forests, the great plains, the rivers, the mountains — and found these plains, these mountains. No force of terror, no pressure of population, drove our ancestors across this continent. They came, as the great explorers crossed the Atlantic, because of the imagination of their minds — because they imagined a better, a more beautiful, a freer, happier world; because they were men not only of courage, not only of strength and hardiness, but of warm and vivid desire; because they desired; because they had the power to desire.

And what was true of the continent was true of the Republic we created. Because our forefathers were able to conceive a free man's government, they were able to create it. Because those who lived before us in this nation were able to imagine a new thing, a thing unheard of in the world before, a thing the skeptical and tired men who did not trust in dreams had not been able to imagine, they erected on this continent the first free nation — the first society in which mankind was to be free at last.

The courage of the Declaration of Independence is a far greater courage than the bravery of those who risked their necks to sign it. The courage of the Declaration of Independence is the courage of the act of the imagination. Jefferson's document is not a call to revolution only. Jefferson's document is an image of a life, a dream — indeed a dream. And yet there were men as careful of their own respect, as hardheaded, as practical, as eager to be thought so, as any now in public life, who signed that Declaration for the world to look at.

The *truth* is that the tradition of imagination is behind us as behind no people in the history of the world. But our right to live as we imagine men should live is not a right drawn from tradition only. There are nations of the earth in which the act of the imagination would be an act *in* the imagination only — an action of escape. But not with us.

We have, and we know we have, the abundant means to bring our boldest dreams to pass — to create for ourselves whatever world we have the courage to desire. We have the metal and the men to take this country down, if we please to take it down, and to build it again as we please to build it. We have the tools and the skill and the intelligence to take our cities apart and to put them together, to lead our roads and rivers where we please to lead them, to build our houses where we want our houses, to brighten the air, to clean the wind, to live as men in this Republic, free men, should be living. We have the power and the courage and the resources of good-will and decency and common understanding — a long experience of decency and common understanding — to enable us to live, not in this continent alone but in the world, as citizens in common of the world, with many others.

We have the power and the courage and the resources of experience to create a nation such as men have never seen. And, more than that, we have the moment of creation in our hands. Our forefathers, when they came to the New England valleys or the Appalachian meadows, girdled the trees and dragged the roots into fences and built themselves shelters and, so roughly housed, farmed the land for their necessities. Then, later, when there were means to do it, when there was time, when the occasion offered, they burned the tangled roots and rebuilt their fences and their houses — but rebuilt them with a difference: rebuilt them as villages, as neighborhoods; rebuilt them with those lovely streets, those schools, those churches which still speak of their conception of the world they wanted. When the means offered, when the time offered, men created, on the clearings of the early useful farms, the towns that made New England and the Alleghenies.

Now is the time for the re-creation, the rebuilding, not of the villages and towns but of a nation. Now is the time to consider that the trees are down, that the land has been broken, that the means are available and the continent itself must be rebuilt. Our necessities have been accomplished as men have always accomplished their necessities — with wastefulness, with ugliness, with cruelty, as well as with the food of harvests. Our necessities have been accomplished with the roots of the broken trees along the fences, the rough shelters, the lonely lives. Now is the time to build the continent itself — to take down and to rebuild; and not the houses and the cities only, but the life itself, raising upon the ready land the brotherhood that can employ it and delight in it and use it as people such as ours should use it.

We stand at the moment of the building of great lives, for the war's end and our victory in the war will throw that moment and the means before us. But to seize the moment and the means we must agree, as men in those New England valleys were agreed, upon the world we mean to bring about. We must agree upon the image of that world.

And this precisely is the thing we have not done and seem incapable of doing. Neither in these years of war nor in the

years before them; never since America became a land of
wealth, a country of abundance, a nation which could bring
its dreams to pass; never since the industrialization of the
continent and the opening of its vast American resources of
men and ore and grain and cloth and cattle — never have
we considered as a people what we meant to be, what
we desired.

When we speak of our ideal conception of ourselves, we
speak still in terms of the agricultural and sparsely settled
nation Thomas Jefferson and his contemporaries had in mind.
The ideal landscape of America which Jefferson painted hangs
unaltered in the American imagination — a clean, small landscape with its isolated figures, its pleasant barns, its self-reliant
rooftrees, its horizons clear of the smoke and the fumes of
cities, its air still, its frontiers protected by month-wide oceans,
year-wide wildernesses. No later hand has touched it, except
Lincoln's maybe, deepening the shadow, widening the sky,
broadening the acreage of the name of freedom, giving the
parts a wholeness that in brighter, sharper light they lacked.
For fifty years and longer it has been a landscape of a world
that no man living could expect to see except behind him, a
landscape no Americans could bring to being, a dream — but
of the past, and not the future.

And yet we keep this image in our minds. This, and not
the world beyond us, is the world we turn to: the lost, nostalgic
image of a world that was the future to a generation dead
a hundred years. No other image has been made to take its
place. No one has dreamed a new American dream of the
new America — the industrial nation of the huge machines,
the limitless earth, the vast and skillful populations, the mountains of copper and iron, the mile-long plants, the delicate
laboratories, the tremendous dams. No one has imagined this
America — what its life should be; what life it should lead

with its great wealth and the tools in its hands and the men
to employ them.

The plants and the factories and their products have been
celebrated often enough — perhaps too often. The statistics
have been added up. The camera has held its mirror to the
great machines. But the central question we have never asked.
What are they *for,* these plants and products, these statistics?
What are they for in terms of a nation of men — in Jefferson's
terms? What is the ideal landscape of this new America?
What are we trying to become, to bring about? What is our
dream of ourselves as a great people? What would we be if we
could: what would our lives be? And how will we use this
skill, this wealth, this power to create those lives?

What is demanded of us in this time of change, what our
whole history and our present need demand of us, is that we
find the answers to these questions — that we consider what
we wish this new America to be. For what we wish to be we
can become.

And if we cannot wish — we shall become that also.

There are men, it is true, who believe there are no answers.
There are men, and among the wisest of our time, who do not
believe that an image of this new America can be conceived —
who do not believe in a world of plenty; do not believe in it
with their hearts whatever their senses tell them; do not
believe that the lives of men can be good lives in the industrialized society which alone makes plenty possible.

Judge Learned Hand spoke not for Mr. Justice Brandeis
alone, but for many others, when he summarized the Justice's
position as resting on the strong belief that "most of our positive ills have directly resulted from great size. With it has
indeed come the magic of modern communication and quick
transport; but out of these has come the sinister apparatus of

mass suggestion and mass production. . . . The herd is regain-
ing its ancient and evil primacy. . . . These many inventions
are a step backward . . . our security has actually diminished
as our demands have become more exacting: our comforts
we purchase at the cost of a softer fiber, a feebler will, and an
infantile suggestibility."

And in the concluding sentences of his noble tribute to
the great Justice, Judge Hand used words which many of the
best of his contemporaries would speak after him without the
alteration of a syllable: "You may build your Tower of Babel
to the clouds; you may contrive ingeniously to circumvent
Nature by devices beyond even the understanding of all but
a handful; you may provide endless distractions to escape
the tedium of your barren lives; you may rummage the whole
planet for your ease and comfort. It shall avail you nothing;
the more you struggle the more deeply you will be enmeshed."

They are eloquent words and noble words. They respond
to a strong strain in the American character. But are they
necessarily and inevitably true? Is it inevitable that men
who contrive ingeniously to circumvent nature should live
tedious and barren lives and fall into the fatness of the spirit
we, as well as Justice Brandeis, have seen and hated? Is
it inconceivable that men should achieve a life with the machines as disciplined and honorable and as free as the life that
Jefferson believed they could achieve with mules and oxen?
Is it certain that the human spirit can survive and flourish only
in a world where need and hardship drive with stinging
whips?

Is the fault with the machines or with ourselves? Is it because we have automobiles to ride in, because we can purchase certain commodities easily, because our presses can
turn out tons of printed paper in a day, that our fiber is soft,
our will feeble, our suggestibility infantile? Or is it because

we do not use these things as we should use them — because
we have not made them serve our moral purpose as a people,
but only contribute to our private comfort as their owners?

Is the whole question indeed not a question of ourselves
instead of our devices? Is it not for us to *say* how these
devices, these inventions, should be used? Does their use not
rest upon the purpose of their use? And does the purpose not
depend upon our power to conceive the purpose — our power
as a people to conceive the purpose of the tools we use;
our power as a people to conceive and to imagine?

A hundred and fifty years ago De Crèvecoeur asked a
famous question which has echoes now: "What then is the
American, this new man?" But what then *is* he? What then
is he now? A man incapable of the act of the imagination or
a man to whom it is native and natural? A man to dare the
dream of plenty with all its risks and dangers, or a man to
hold to the old nostalgic landscape with the simple virtues
safely forced upon him by the necessary self-denial?

A man who has the courage to think a nation may have
physical abundance and still retain, or still not lose, its soul?
Or a man to accept the shamefaced verdict of the twenty years
just past and return to the discipline of want and hunger?

A man who has the hardihood or the courage to believe that
the machines which have enslaved his fathers will make his
children free — free as no human beings in the world have
yet known freedom; free of the twisting miseries and hungers;
free to become themselves? Or a man to reject the hope of that
enfranchised freedom and to seek his independence in the
ancient narrow circle of his old dependence on himself?

Which of these two men is the American? We should have
said a while ago we knew. We should have said the American
character was self-evident: A restless man. A great builder
and maker and shaper, a man delighting in size and height and

dimensions: the world's tallest; the town's biggest. A man never satisfied — never — with anything: his house or the town where his grandfather settled or his father's profession or even his own, for that matter. An inveterate voyager and changer and finder. A man naturally hopeful; a believing man, believing that things progress, that things get forwarder. A skillful man with contraptions of one kind and another — machines, engines, various devices: familiar with all of them. A man of certain unquestioned convictions — of a strong, natural attachment to certain ideas and to certain ideals. But first of all and foremost of all a restless man and a believing man, a builder and changer of things and of nations.

We should have said, a generation back, there was no possible doubt or question of the will and power of this nation to propose the kind of future for itself which would employ the means of plenty for a human purpose. We should have said the principal characteristic of the American people was a confidence in the future and themselves — confidence that the future was the thing they'd make it. I cannot think, for myself, we have so changed that we do not believe this now. I cannot believe we are so changed that we'll let ourselves go with the drag and the current of history — that we'll let the future happen to us as the future happens to chips on a river or sheep in a blizzard; that we'll let the peace make us: not us the peace. I cannot believe we have so changed that we do not believe in ourselves and the future.

And yet we have not done what must be done if we believe the future is the thing we'll make it. We have not named that future.

And the time is short.

It is many years since Matthew Arnold saw his generation standing between two worlds, one dead, the other waiting to be born. Our time is still the time between these worlds; and the wars we suffer, the disasters, the uneasiness, are natural to the time we live in like the continuing and violent storms that drive the days between the seasons. We shall not have peace in truth, peace for our lives, peace for the purposes of our lives, until the world we wait for has been born. But it will not be born until we recognize it, until we shape it with our expectation and our hope. The new worlds do not bring themselves to being. Men's minds, when they are ready for them, find them. The labor and the longing must be ours.

They must be ours as men and also — and this is the truth our generation in this country must accept — as Americans. For the future is America's to make. It is not our future, as a few Americans have asked us to believe, to master or exploit. It is not an American future for some vast imperial enterprise, some huge dominion of the earth or sky. And yet it is our future. It is ours to shape. It is ours to shape, not because we have many planes or great numbers of ships or rich industrial resources but for a different reason: because we have the power as a people to conceive so great a future as mankind must now conceive — because we have behind us a tradition of imagination in the people.

But because we have the power we have also a responsibility to use the power. While there still is time.

1943

3

Notes on the Image of Man in These Mornings

The act of recognition is the act of art — the collision between the expectation and the image.

3

NOTES ON THE IMAGE OF MAN IN
THESE MORNINGS

These notes have been copied, with occasional changes
in the interest of intelligibility, from a dozen or so note-
books of all sizes and colors which I kept from the time
I stopped practising law in 1923 to the time I entered the
government service in 1938 (one or two entries from
the years since can be identified by subject matter).

They reflect a time which seems far away now —
unbelievably far, I thought, as I worked through the
books. But some at least of the questions which concerned us then, and which we used to talk about afternoons on the sidewalks, are questions still and probably
will continue to be as long as men make new beginnings.

THERE IS A NEW IMAGE OF MAN in our time which many of
us have dreamed but none seen though Perse almost brings it
to vision in *Anabase*. Rivera's frescoes in the little chapel
out across the lake bed (in Mexico) catch a refracted glimpse
of it from the corner of the eye. It is true that no whole man
can live on the Communist dog biscuit. It is true also that
these frescoes betray the synthetic diet. But there is something
else too. One says: What new dignity of man is this? Merely
the noble savage repainted as the noble peasant or the noble
pulque-drinker or the noble welder? Or something more?
And one answers: Something more — and wonders how this

33

guessed-at figure of mankind can move our generation of mor-
bidly swollen egos with the reddened eyes and weeping faces.
How can such men and women as we are find the image of our
lives in the odor of labor and sun and a love simple and violent
as the habit of the heart? How can this image be *feasible* to us?
It makes a man *less* and *real* and we do not wish to be either.
We wish to be *each*. We are determined to be *each* — never
guessing that we must buy that right.

The ego is the great lie falsifying everything universal and
true. But it is also the one great truth — the one true universal. The particulars — what clothes, wives, money, looks —
vary from man to man. Only I Myself am in everyone, and
in each one I.

The soul is indeed as silly as Chaucer said it was. Without
the habit of the senses to go with it and surround it, it stands
gawking at the world incapable of anything but joy and terror.
It happens to all of us to waken out of sleep without our lives
around us; to waken "before our memories," and to stand
naked not only in the body but the soul, our two hands nosing
at our flanks like dogs at a strange cadaver, unable to *place*
ourselves, to *recognize* ourselves. There is a bathroom still
in a house on Bowdoin Street in Cambridge where the grey
light of a winter morning is reflected in a mirror that should
have held my face but held instead a face I'd never seen — a
face I *did not remember* ever having seen.

The mystery is that there should be a mystery — that we
do not accept without even a thought of questioning. Is it
because we were once accustomed to understand and now
understand no longer? Or is it because the world has an *air*
of meaning — as though it were *about* to tell?

In poetry as in anything else a decent regard for one's own dignity as a human being — at least in one's own eyes — is commendable. There is no substitute for self-respect. Not the kind of preoccupation with himself which keeps a man from hearing and seeing and feeling, but a proper concern for the judgments of his own soul — and the courage to hear them. Remembering that very few of the judgments of the world are half as knowledgeable or half as disinterested as the things one *really* thinks about oneself, oneself — but tries not to overhear. ". . . people listen," said Gide, "to the advice of others with much less effort and hence more willingly than they listen to their own." Let the philosophers and the philistines ask life to tell them who they are. The poet's question is the opposite. It takes gall to ask it.

Also there are certain questions only a poem can ask. Why, weeping, do you lean your head against mine? Do I not also weep?

Schopenhauer speaks as a philosopher and a moralist when he says that the artist is under a duty to present the universe as he himself sees it. "His peculiar view of the universe." Why? The universe remains. It is there for anyone to see. And what is it precisely that an artist leaves behind him when he puts it down that This is beautiful, This is sad, This is like this, This other is like this other — when he puts it down that his life comes up out of sleep as a bough lifts when the snow slides from it? What is it that he puts down? What is it that all artists from the beginning have put down in the many records? Images of the universe or images of themselves?

What we know as the universe is an infinitely slow explosion of the seeds of matter like that flowering cloud over

Bikini Atoll which burst from loveliness into loveliness out of the huge collision of the lagoon and hung there and faded. Form bursts from form into form but the whole is one form which the timeless eye can see — the eye outside of time — the eye outside of the explosion which is time. It is this eye outside of time that poetry is always seeking. Aristotle was wrong when he made poetry a mirror. Poetry is not a mirror of time for time to look in. Such a mirror would not show the movement *past* which gives the world its meaning. Poetry is a point outside of time — or rather, it is a search for a point outside of time — a point from which time may be seen. The task is still

> . . . to poise
> Eternity upon the turning pole.

But the problem of form and the problem of perception are very closely related. It is not a question of perceiving and then finding the words for the perception. I suspect that most poets perceive *in words*. Or in images that are at once forms of words. "The moon cocked its old white head in the sky and listened to the dogs barking." To write at all one must be capable of seeing objects in a relation to each other and to time which makes them *appear*. But appear in words.

The trouble with life? The trouble with life is that about the time you begin to think what the trouble with life is you begin to find out. And about the time you begin to find out you find out that life has lost interest in *you*. Turned its back on you. Like this day (at Granville) of off-shore wind with the sounds of the rail-road yard and the faint yelping of dogs and Ada's voice high and pure and sweet singing the Chant Dissident of Stravinsky all blown out and away from me out to sea and the shoulders of the little waves running

backward up the slope of the sea away from me with their
bundles of white in their arms leaving nothing behind but me
here at this table and an empty page and a white butterfly
falling falling falling toward the sea. Turns its back on you!

What makes you desperate is the way the world keeps
looking at you as though you ought to understand. Like a
woman in an evening dress with her hair brushed back hard
over her ears and her dress drawn down tight over her sig-
nificant bosom humming at you, with closed lips, the same
thing over and over, never quite right, her eyes looking at you
intelligently and brightly as though you would certainly remember the words, poet that you are. And you don't.

Yeats had much the same hatred of dead phrases and gen-
eralizations, though he attributed the ills of contemporary
speech to "the scientific movement" and to "newspaper government." The language which now afflicts us, he says, is a
language made by "minds that would grasp what they have
never seen." In the old days it was not so. Men in that time
wrote "out of their own rich experience . . ." Which is all
very well, and true enough, except that some of the deadest
and most literary language is to be found precisely in the
work of these people who wrote "out of their own rich experience." And the further fact that Yeats himself says in the
same book: ". . . I . . . who have never observed anything or
listened with an attentive ear. . . ."

Or maybe Colonel de Brémond was right that day at the
beginning of the second battle of the Marne when I parked
the battery trucks in a crooked line and he yelled at me and
I shouted back: "Sir, the trouble is . . ." and he walked across
in front of the guns and looked at me hard and said: "The

trouble is that there *is* no trouble. The trouble is always *you!*
Never forget it." (Colonel de Brémond is dead thirty years
but I never have.)

Cummings and John Bishop in the glass porch at St. Cloud
delighting themselves with a mock-literary conversation. The
difference between prose and poetry is . . . Anything is poetry
which suffers if the lines are run together. The important
thing is the blank space at the end of the line. Prose is ar-
ranged perpendicularly: poetry horizontally. Cummings with
that glinting, solemn grin of his: John whinnying off into his
Trojan laugh. There was never a charm at once as taking
and as withheld as Cummings' or a nature more generous and
sensitive than John's. Or a city that became them both better
than Paris in that year.

At first the chronicles were written in poetry: then in prose,
leaving to poetry the fictions. Then the fictions were written
in prose leaving to poetry the mirrors. Then prose invaded the
mirrors. Leaving to poetry, itself. Cannibal flower devouring
its own leaves. Poems constructed out of the rubble of de-
serted poems. The horse-hair tents among the pillars at
Persepolis where the nomads, driven from the cities, leave
messages for each other spelled out in pieces of broken marble.

It is not the art of poetry alone which has suffered by this
great invasion and conquest of prose. Men have suffered
also. For prose is not an easier and more efficient way of
recording experience. When the past was recorded in the
great poetic chronicles, it was recorded as a metaphor of
man's life. Now that it is recorded in prose it is recorded as
history — truer and yet less true — truer to the "facts" and
yet less true to the meaning of the facts. Sooner or later it

will become necessary to turn the vast and complicated volume of prose history back into myth to give it meaning.

Why is Toynbee read by thousands who struggle painfully to understand? Because they guess, even without understanding, that unless the vast prose of our civilization is turned back, and turned back quickly, into myth there will be no civilization left. It may be that the wheel has come 'round again and that it is we who do not know it — we who regret the state of poetry in our time.

The uses of poetry? Let those who wonder consider the wind. What is it that seizes a tree and sways it and lets it go? We say "the wind" and do not think of it anymore and therefore do not see it anymore. Air daffing at the green skin of the earth, curling under the dust in a wall's shelter, blurring the water away out. If we had not hidden it under a name we would see the marvel of its movement. What poetry does is to dissolve the name and reveal the thing, naked and beautiful.

It is not the poet's part to impose order by fiat like a ruler, or by argument like a philosopher, or by faith like a saint, but to discover it. If it exists and where it exists and not otherwise. Even though he finds it in its opposite as Empedocles did who said that the universe exists by virtue of the discord of its elements and that if harmony were to take the place of discord the universe would disrupt into chaos.

Yeats says somewhere that at about thirty "any writer who is anything of an artist comes to understand that all a work of art can do is to show us the reality that is within our minds and the reality that our eyes look on." Why "all?" What more is there? The act of recognition is the act of art — the collision between the expectation and the image. The way, in autumn, in a still river, a leaf will detach itself from the depth of the mirror and fall over and over upward until it meets, with a minute shock and trembling of water, its descending self upon the surface of the glass.

The morbid preoccupation with *novelty* in my generation. Pound's title, *Make It New,* was the sacred slogan. We should have realized, simply by taking note of the nature of the preoccupation, that the trouble lay deeper. Any professional writer knows that when he finds himself confused to the point of frustration by the problem of saying what he thinks he wants to say, the trouble is generally with what he thinks he wants to say, not with the form in which he thinks he wants to say it. Our trouble was with what we thought we wanted our poems to show us. The world, we thought, was new. But in what way it was new we were by no means clear. Eliot knew very well what he thought he wanted to see and the result was *The Waste Land.* Though a very different world. No good poem was ever written *to be different.*

Tiberius spoke for us all when he said: "And how am I to restore the simplicity of ancient times?"

The test of a poem is not its power to create emotion but to withstand emotion.

The insistence that a poem must move the reader emotionally is merely another form of the notion that art must have an excuse — to teach, to elevate, to move. It is no rare thing to have emotions and it is not hard to make others have them. But to write a poem is another thing. The relation of emotion to poetry is not the relation of end to means but the reverse. The end of a poem is to exist as a poem. Emotion is the means by which the poem is made to exist *as a poem* where alone it can so exist — in the mind of the reader or hearer.

Also there are doors out of time like the door in the south porch of the Cathedral of Bourges opening slowly to the coffin and the little company of the living which surrounded it, showing for a moment the cold square of winter sunlight in a watery sky and closed again.

1948

4

The Definition of Victory

We can make it clear to the whole world . . . that those who live by contempt for the people will die by contempt for the people — that it is the people . . . to whom the future really belongs.

4

THE DEFINITION OF VICTORY

IT IS ALL VERY WELL to think of victory as a symbolic winged figure without face or arms, an abstract, soaring shape of military triumph, to be followed by the dull business of negotiating peace. But a soldiers' triumph cannot serve a people's war. The people wish to end their wars, not merely win them. And the victories that end the wars are not the headless marble victories of winged fame. The victories that end the wars have human attributes. Those who win them — those who deserve to win them and so win them — are those who dare to look them in the face, however dark that face may be, and so to recognize them, and so to recognize no other.

We citizens of the United States and our allies in Great Britain and elsewhere have not learned to recognize the face of the victory we mean to win to end this war. We have not answered the questions which must be answered. And the consequence is the curious anxiety, the strange concern, with which we move toward victory. We are like a man running a race with all his determination, all his reserves of energy and strength, who does not know whether the race will be won when he passes his adversary, or when his adversary drops out, or when he himself reaches a given mark — and, if so, where that mark is fixed. He sees his adversary tiring. He is certain his adversary can be defeated. But he does not know in what way the race itself is to be won or whether indeed it can be won at all. He only knows that he has no choice but to run this race and that he dare not lose it.

Why we find ourselves in this state of inconclusiveness it is not difficult I think to say. We have waited for the war itself to define our victory by yielding it. We have been unwilling to face the essential, the elementary fact, that this war, unlike some other wars, does not carry in itself the measure of its failure or success — that we ourselves must invent, must create, that measure — that only by an affirmative act of purpose and of will can we determine what the measure of success will be. In other wars — some other wars — the cause of war determines almost automatically the definition of the end. The war is won when the disputed city is captured. In this war the beginning does not define the end. We went to war because the entire security of our lives, moral and physical, was threatened by an armed attack first upon our neighbors' lives and then upon our own. But we are not fighting merely to defeat the attackers in their effort to overrun the world. We are fighting to establish the future security of the moral and physical life for the defense of which we took up arms. Which means that the war which was at first defensive on our part has now become offensive. Which means, in turn, that we ourselves must fix our goal and our objective — that we ourselves, by an act of will, by an act of decision, must determine what the end will be.

We may find it preposterous to be asked what we propose to do about the beliefs of the Germans and the Japanese, but we are asked notwithstanding. We are asked by the mouths of innumerable men and women who have been destroyed in two wars within a single generation because the people of Germany believed the strong should inherit the earth — believed it so violently that when they were disarmed they created for themselves out of their hunger and their poverty new arms more dangerous than any they had lost before. We are asked by the mouths of boys who have rotted in jungles and perished in prison camps and been murdered on hospital litters and suffered physical torture and spiritual indignity because the people of Japan believe they are a superior people entitled by right to conquer the world and to do what they please with whatever opposes them. We may find it preposterous to be asked what we propose to do about the belief of the people of Germany and the people of Japan, but we know if we know anything that it is the belief of the German people and the Japanese people which is dangerous to us — not their armies or their industries or their ships or planes. For the malicious purpose can create the arms and armies out of nothing as we ourselves have seen, but the arms and armies without the malicious purpose are no more dangerous than Canada's across the open border — less dangerous, because farther off.

If we are honest with ourselves and with what we know, we will not refuse to face the truth because it is difficult. We will not pretend to ourselves, what we know in fact to be false, that this war can be won — which means that this war can be ended — by the defeat of armies in the field alone. This war can be ended only by destroying the will which made it, as well as the weapons with which that will was armed. We will never believe again — if we are honest with ourselves we will never believe again — that when the weapons are destroyed the will is destroyed also. We know better. Or if we don't we have only ourselves to blame.

Neither, if we are honest with ourselves, will we exaggerate the difficulty of the destruction of the fascist will. The fascist will can be destroyed, as the President said, by destroying the philosophy on which it rests. And the destruction of a false philosophy is neither more nor less difficult than any other cleansing labor. Because those who have attempted to destroy philosophies by suppressing them, or by persecuting those who hold them, have failed and rightly failed, it does not follow that the philosophies which mislead the world are indestructible. There is one unfailing method by which even the most powerful, the most persuasive, of the false beliefs can be destroyed — by discrediting their claims to truth. What persecution cannot do and suppression cannot do, the naked truth can do when men are made to see it. The methods of the Spanish Inquisition had little effect upon the European mind, but Erasmus, by discrediting the pretensions of the Schoolmen, altered the thinking of the western world for generations.

We can win this war in terms not only of the disarming of our enemies but in terms also of the destruction of their philosophy, if we win it in such a way as to discredit that philosophy — in such a way as to demonstrate to the people of Germany and Japan, and to those in other countries who, secretly or openly, have emulated Japanese and German beliefs, that these beliefs are false and, worse than false, contemptible.

But this we must do, if we are to do it, in the act of winning the war, and as part of the winning of the war.

No one seriously believes that the United Nations will undertake the de-indoctrination of the German and Japanese people by a generation's supervision of German and Japanese schools. But no one can doubt either that what cannot be taught in a generation of school keeping can be taught, if we mean to teach it, in a single military defeat. It is when we think of the destruction of the Nazi philosophy in terms of a peace to be negotiated and enforced after the war that the problem becomes insoluble. It can be solved only by thinking of it in terms of the war itself, in terms of the victory which we mean to win. For the philosophy of our enemies is a philosophy exceedingly vulnerable to precisely such a refutation as our victory can be made to give.

What must be destroyed in the philosophy of our enemies — what is hateful and menacing in that philosophy and must be destroyed — is not its aspiration to power. The desire for power is a very ancient and a very general human desire and one which has produced in its time both good and evil. What is hateful and menacing in the philosophy of our enemies, and what must be discredited in the defeat which brings them down, is the contempt for humanity, the contempt for human life, the contempt for the human life of individual men and women, which makes their aspiration to power a brutal and horrible aspiration, destructive of every human decency, of every human basis for a common life. The principal evil Nazism has done — an evil far greater than the Nazi bombing of undefended cities and the Nazi strafing of unprotected civilians — is the Nazi destruction in millions of young German minds, and in the minds of other millions in other countries who are susceptible to the Nazi infection, of belief in humanity, of respect for man. Mr. Roosevelt was profoundly right when he told the Congress in January 1943 that "The issue of this war is the basic issue between those who believe in mankind and those who do not — the ancient issue between those who put their faith in the people and those who put their faith in dictators and tyrants."

That *is* the issue. It is an issue moreover — and this is our great good fortune if we wish to use it — which the outcome of this war can go a great way to adjudicate. Had our enemies won, they would have employed every means at their disposal to drive home the corollary that governments which put their trust in the people, governments which represent the people, governments which are the people, cannot survive in competition with governments which govern the people, governments which "discipline" the people — governments in brief which despise the people. Now that it is apparent that our enemies will not win, we can, if we please, drive home the very different lesson which our victory can be made to demonstrate. We can make it clear to the whole world, and not to the Nazis and the Japanese alone, that the people won this war against the despisers of the people — that the people's governments and the people's armies were more powerful, and always will be, than the armies of the slave states and the tyrant dominions — that belief in the people is a strength not to be gainsaid, and contempt for the people an inevitable and a fatal weakness — that those who live by contempt for the people will die by contempt for the people — that it is the people and not the enemies of the people to whom the future really belongs.

We *can* do this. But we can do it only if we mean to do it. It will not follow automatically from our military victory alone, however overwhelming our military victory may be. It will not be accomplished by any application of the simple smoking-room proposition that "this time we will march to Berlin." Where we march is less important than the way we march there. We can only prove that our victory is a victory for the people by making it a victory for the people. And words will not supply the proof though words will help. There should be words now — there should have been words before now — declaring again and again that this is no longer a war of resisting nations against aggressor nations — that this is a war now of the people's governments against the tyrant governments, of the people's armies against the slave armies, of the people's belief in themselves against the fascists' contempt for the people — that what is at stake in this war is a great principle, the principle won in the people's revolutions of the past one hundred and fifty years, the principle that the people can govern themselves and of right should. There ought to be words to say not once but many times that this war is a war fought in vindication of the principle of those revolutions and to secure the gains they won and to extend them.

But words alone will not do what must be done. There must be action also. And the acts must accord with the words. The acts must demonstrate that the allied governments are in truth the people's governments, that our armies are in fact the people's armies, and that the principle for which we fight is indeed the principle of the defense and vindication and extension of the people's revolutions of 1775 and 1789 and 1824 and 1848 and the people's years thereafter. For if our words declare, and if our actions demonstrate, that this war is a people's war in vindication of the people's revolutions, then our victory in this war will become what it must become if the war is to be ended and so won. It will become the final and unanswerable proof that the philosophy of our enemies — the philosophy of contempt and cynicism — is itself contemptible and false. It will become not a military victory alone but a victory in the more enduring world of principle. It will become a victory which not only disarms our enemies, but discredits what they practised and believed.

To define our victory in these terms before our victory shall be half won and so irreparably lost is the desperate necessity of these months.

1943

5

The Definition of Peace

Is the peace we mean the armed peace, the war without warfare, the peace that devours the peace-makers, bleeding them white, rotting their liberties, raising the stones themselves of the earth to hate them?

5

THE DEFINITION OF PEACE
Christmas, 1943

THIS IS THE DAY dedicated throughout the Western World
to peace. This is a day of war also — like another. It is not
strange or inappropriate that we should dedicate a day of
war to peace. Nevertheless, the war that changes everything
changes this day also. There is an irony in the talk of peace
in time of war that edges the familiar words until they wound
us. This is the day of peace, the words say. But to us they
say, One day out of how many days? And of what peace?

When we speak to each other of peace in the welter of
blood and of agony in which the world now lives — of men
dying day after day in unimaginable numbers and by every
death — by mutilation with iron, by drowning at sea, by
calculated torture, by cold, heat, hunger, disease — by every
death by which men have died before and by many deaths
unknown until this generation — when we use the words for
peace to each other in this time of war, the irony answers us:
what peace?

Is it the old lethargic peace we mean, the peace of the
'twenties and 'thirties, the peace that lasts from one war till
the next? Is the peace we mean, the peace of those who say,
Sufficient unto the day is the evil thereof? Is the peace we
mean the peace of those who used to tell us, If we leave them
alone they'll leave us alone; of those who used to tell us, It
takes two to make a war; of those who used to say, The

55

Atlantic is three thousand miles across and the Pacific is broader; of those who used to sit back in the soft seats of the afternoon automobiles and refuse to be bothered? Is it this peace, the fatuous peace, the irresponsible peace, the peace that has killed more men in the last four years than the warmakers — is it this we mean when we talk about peace on this Christmas?

Or is it another peace we mean? Is it the new peace the wise men are starting to talk about now that the war will be won? Is it the new peace of the hard-headed men who know what the score is: who know all the answers? — the new peace of those who are learning to say that God helps those who help themselves; that God's on the side of the heavy battalions? Is it the peace of those who tell us the best treaty of peace is the biggest Navy; of those who say, If the oceans aren't wide enough widen the oceans; of those who say, Grab for the bases, Hang onto the islands, Buy up the airways, Build a fence to the stratosphere, Lock the gate, Kick the foreigners out and lock the gate after them? Is it the hard-headed peace, the strong-arm peace, the loud-mouthed peace, the peace that is war in suspense, war without motion — the lasting peace that will last while the gun is aimed, while the Army is ready to march, while the bombers are ready — is it this we mean by peace in the year of Tarawa, in the year of Salerno, in the year of the Russian dead and the dead of the deserts? Is the peace we mean the armed peace, the war without warfare, the peace that devours the peace-makers, bleeding them white, rotting their liberties, raising the stones themselves of the earth to hate them? Is it peace by the sword and to end by the sword we mean?

We have heard the word both ways in the time we live in. We have heard the fatuous speech about peace being something that comes of itself if you hate war hard enough,

something you get without effort or struggle by wanting it —
the way the Dutch and Norwegians got it by wanting it. We
have heard the realistic speech about peace being something
you get if you're strong and you take it, something you get with
a whip like a tiger's obedience — the way the Nazis have
got it in Norway and Holland — the way the hard-headed
men have always got it — and lost it — losing themselves and
their nations.

And which do we mean? Which will we say we mean to
the young men living and dead who deserve to know what
we mean? Shall we tell them the peace we mean is the armed
peace, the peace imposed at the point of a gun by an army of
millions? Shall we tell them the peace we mean is the fat
peace, the negligent peace, the slumbering peace of the automobiles on the Sunday afternoons in the croon of the radios —
the peace that comes of itself without effort — and goes without effort?

Or is there a different peace we mean when the irony cuts
at us? Is there a peace of which we can speak without shame
to those who have died for peace, as we've told them, and
those who have not yet died? Is there a peace that a man can
speak of with honesty facing the millions living and those
dead?

It is there that the irony cuts at us most when we talk of
peace on this Christmas. We know that the young who die will
die because we did not make a peace before when the last
war ended. We know that the young who die will die to buy
us a second chance to make a peace. We know that when
we talk of peace they remember this. The word has the taste
of shame in our mouths when we speak it.

It is right we should feel shame. We are a generation guilty
of two wars within twenty years, and the second we could
have prevented with wisdom and courage. We are a generation

which failed to make the peace we owed to the dead of one
world war — who were our brothers: and we talk now of
peace to the living and dead of another war — who are our
sons.

But nevertheless if we are a guilty generation we are
fortunate also. We have learned what our failure was while
the chance of action remains to us. Time that does not often
return to the things done and the things not done has returned
for us. What we failed before to do from sickness of heart
and from lethargy, letting the old men trick us with their
tempters' talk of a world reverting to normalcy — what we
failed to do out of folly and falsehoods before, time has given
us one more chance to do.

And we know what must be done. We know that peace
must be *made*. We know that peace is a thing to be *made,*
not accepted; a thing to be *made,* not reduced to a treaty on
paper; a thing to be *made* as a city is made, as anything great
and difficult is made, by labor, by labor in common, by labor
in common of all whom it touches, by continuing labor, increasing labor, labor that does not end with a meeting or conference, labor that does not limit itself to a few men in a
room at a table, labor of peoples, labor of nations.

We have talked about making peace before but peace has
never been *made* in the world's history. Peace has been put
upon paper. Peace has been faked with a great Army and
Navy enforcing fear. But peace has never been made in
human history as a positive thing, a created thing, a thing that
the peoples create, and in common, to serve them, a positive
structure and fabric of common peace constructed by labor
in common of science and learning for life's sake and for hope
in it.

Our generation knows, as no generation before it has ever
known, that peace must be *made*. Our generation knows that

it will have its second chance to make a peace. If we mean when we talk of peace on this Christmas that peace will in truth be made when the war is won — that nothing this time will stop us from making peace — that neither lies nor deceptions nor tricks nor our own weariness will prevent us — if we mean this we can speak of peace to the living and dead without shame. If we do not mean it — if it is less than this we mean — if we mean it with reservations, with caution, with carefulness — then let us in common decency be quiet and not talk of peace. For nothing is true or honest in the talk of peace but our own purpose. And the choice is ours.

December 25, 1943

6

Indian Summer

We have been living . . . in a kind of Indian Summer of history: an unreal time.

6

INDIAN SUMMER

OCTOBER IN NEW ENGLAND was a parable. For more than three weeks the days turned slowly in an enchanted stillness of blue overhead, gold underfoot. The trees held their foliage or let it fall little by little from motionless branches and the sun at noon was hot in the high silence. Evenings you could hear the door of a car close a mile away up the valley and the motor start and a voice lift a little over the sound. There were big stars and no wind, only the drifts of warm air and cool air from the folds of the land smelling of bracken. It was perfect weather or weather as nearly perfect as living men have ever seen. And nevertheless there was no quiet in it. Even before the brush fires started in the pines you felt a sense of tragic imminence, of waiting. October is the time for change and the change had not come. You lay in the hot sun in the dry leaves and took no pleasure in the unreal season.

It was a parable all of us understand very well in America. We have been living for months past in a kind of Indian Summer of history: an unreal time. We are richer as a nation than we have ever been, and stronger and more secure from enemies a man can see. Our national income is far above the figures wise men used to dismiss as fantastic, and our military strength is supported, for the moment at least, by a monopoly of the most formidable weapon ever developed by human beings. And, nevertheless, our minds are not upon our wealth or our strength. We do not believe in the golden weather. We believe instead that the time is a time of conflict and of change, and we talk of the change, which has not yet come, and of the conflict which is obscure and withheld but certain.

It is a curious state of mind in a great people at the moment — as we are continually reminding ourselves — of our fullest greatness. It is also a dangerous state of mind. To lose confidence in peace is to lose the will to peace, and to accept the inevitability of disaster is to cease to resist disaster. As long as men have faith in the possibility of peace, as we did during the war, peace is possible regardless of the legal and political and institutional difficulties. When men come to believe that conflict is inevitable, as we do now, no structure of laws or of institutions can create a peaceful world.

The fundamental question for our time, therefore — a question far more fundamental and immediate than the reform of the structure of the United Nations or its replacement by a different organization — is the source and origin of the sense of fatality which haunts our generation throughout the world and not least in the United States. Why do we believe, with a sullen and resentful but unquestioning conviction, that the time in which we find ourselves is an unreal time, an improbable and belated season which will vanish overnight when the wind changes? Why do we assume that the words *Russia* and *the United States, Capitalism* and *Communism,* in their inevitable pairs, necessarily mean hatred and conflict and in the end, if not catastrophe and war, at least an armed and a divided world?

It is not an easy question to answer even for the fanatical. Nothing has *happened* in the external and visible world to make conflict between the United States and Russia inevitable. Russia has done a number of things which have made Americans understandably apprehensive and Russian officials have spoken a number of words which have made American listeners angry with good reason. The United States, for its part, has taken certain steps which have aroused Russian anxiety, and American speakers and writers, some of them men of present or former responsibility, have published words which have excited proper and indignant reactions in the Soviet Union. But no reasonable and objective man would suggest that anything Mr. Vishinsky or his American competitors have yet said, or anything Washington or Moscow has yet done, would justify the conclusion that war is probable.

Why then must we believe in war? There are two common answers which are, in effect, two forms of the same answer. We must believe in war, say the partisans on the one side or the other, not because of what has already happened in the past but because of what is going to happen in the future. War is inevitable because the future is inevitable. Russia will be compelled to do this or the United States will be compelled to do that and war will inevitably follow. Capitalism has no choice but to become this, or Communism has no choice but to become that, and the ineluctible consequence will be war. According to one view the war will be a war of imperialistic aggression on the model of the imperialist wars of the last century and the beginning of this. According to another the war will be an ideological war on the model of the wars of religion. According to both views war is inescapable unless one side or the other, one dogma or the other, backs down.

In order to understand, therefore, why war must be regarded as all but inevitable in spite of the fact that nothing has yet occurred which reasonable men would consider a cause of war, it is necessary to examine both opinions. The first, which foresees a war of imperialistic aggression, though common enough in certain quarters in the United States, has found its most authoritative and official expression in the Manifesto issued by the eighteen Communist functionaries who met in Poland to establish the so-called Cominform. The second, though standard Communist dogma down to the Polish Manifesto, has achieved its most practical interpretation in the Truman Doctrine and its most enthusiastic reception in certain circles in the Congress of the United States.

The Polish Manifesto, once its mirror-image vocabulary has been mastered, is a brutally simple and explicit document. "Democracy" must be read to mean Communist dictatorship, and "the strengthening of democracy" to refer to the ministrations of the Red Army, but the argument, granted the false-face of its words, is clear enough. Fundamental changes, say the eighteen functionaries, have taken place in the international situation brought about by the Second World War. "The characteristic aspect of these changes is a new balance of political forces interplaying in the world arena . . ." This new balance is expressed in "two camps" which now divide the world. One of these camps is composed of "democratic countries" which "aim at whittling down imperialism and the strengthening of democracy" while the other aims "at the strengthening of imperialism and choking democracy." This second camp shows "a growing aggressive activity" and makes use of a complex "arsenal of tactical weapons" which combine "direct threats of force, blackmail and intimidation, all sorts of political tricks and economic pressure, bribery, the using for its own ends of conflicting interests and disagreements with the aim of strengthening its position." In the face of this attack, the functionaries conclude, all right-thinking men must "grasp in their hands the banner of national independence and sovereignty" and courageously "guard over the democracy, national sovereignty, independence and self-determination of their countries."

As a piece of propaganda for Russian and Balkan consumption this declaration undoubtedly has merits which escape more critical eyes, but as a statement of the reasons for believing in war it cannot fail to disappoint even its most credulous readers. Not only are the roles reversed and the parts mis-labeled but the fundamental thesis is patently false. It would be false with the parts properly distributed and the epithets correctly applied. The one thing certain about the crisis of the contemporary world is the fact that it cannot be explained in nationalistic terms — however useful those terms may have become to the defense of the Soviet position in the Security Council. If our generation had nothing to worry about but the nationalistic rivalries of Russia and the United States, we could sleep at night. Two years of the most assiduous effort by some of the most malicious minds in the two countries have left unaltered the plain and palpable fact that the national interests of the United States and Russia conflict *as national interests* at very few places on the earth's surface — and conflict at these places, not as present and necessary causes of war but as future points of friction in the event of war's occurring. The present "divergence" between the two countries, as Secretary Marshall has put it, "is not due to any direct clash between the national interests of these powers."

Russia and the United States, as nations, as governments, are, it is true, the actors in the tragic play. At the moment they are the principal actors, blustering and bellowing and gesturing at each other in a clown's performance which would be slap-stick farce if it were not played upon the graves of so many men, some dead, some yet to die. But anyone who believes that this farce is the tragedy of our time — anyone who believes that the peoples of the United States and Russia, having learned at such terrible cost to hate war, have been brought in the short space of two years to contemplate the possibility of another war solely by reason of their national rivalry — anyone who believes this has thought very little about the springs of human action.

The second theory, the theory of the religious war, substitutes systems of ideas for nations, and expansion by proselytizing for expansion by imperialism. It is not because Russia is Russia and the United States is the United States that conflict is inevitable but because Russia is Communist and the United States Capitalist and because Communism and Capitalism cannot both survive in the same world. This theory, which had long been attributed to the Communist hierarchy, received official American approval in a curious way. Either as the result of a now famous report by Mr. George F. Kennan, then the director of the Policy Planning Staff of the State Department, or as the result of the presentation of opinions similar to Mr. Kennan's, the American Government adopted the view that if Soviet foreign policy was based, as Mr. Kennan said it was, upon the incompatibility of Capitalism and Communism, then the best way to meet Soviet foreign policy was to anticipate it by declaring open international war upon Communism. This procedure had the added advantage of assuring Congressional support for a policy which might have been suspect had it been presented in the usual diplomatic terms. Conservative passions in the United States are aroused not by Russia as a nation but by Russia as the Communist party. Communism is not feared because it serves the purposes of Russian aggression; Russian aggression is feared because it serves to spread Communism. To strike at Communism directly, therefore, was to establish a policy which, it was hoped, would be effective abroad and popular at home.

The consequences of the enunciation of the Truman Doctrine were not, however, what had been anticipated either at home or abroad. A conservative Congress reacted as it had been expected to react though with rather less enthusiasm than had been hoped for, but the country as a whole was cool and the rest of the world — even the non-Communist rest of the world — was troubled and disturbed. It was not that Communism was popular but that the open declaration of a religious war was unpopular, from whichever side it emanated. It did not correspond to the realities as those realities presented themselves to the great masses of mankind. The bigots and the fanatics at the two extremes might believe in religious war but no one else did. The American Government had never before declared war upon an idea no matter how hateful, and the spectacle was shocking and not a little offensive to a great many Americans who detested Communism quite as warmly as the professional patrioteers. One did not need to look much beyond the face of Congressman J. Parnell Thomas to imagine the effect of such a declaration upon American liberties at home. Its effect upon America's classic foreign policy, which had always aimed at the realization of a world in which, as in the Republic itself, diversities of faith and belief need not necessarily mean war, was only too obvious.

What the demise of the Truman Doctrine and the substitution of the Marshall Plan means in terms of the future position of the United States is not yet clear and will not be clear until the Marshall Plan is put into effect. What it means, however, in terms of the theory of religious war, is evident. There is no such inevitable conflict — no such inescapable either-or — as the Soviet priesthood had prophesied and the American Government acknowledged. Neither in men's minds, nor in the external world of happenings and events, is the choice between Capitalism and Communism an inescapable choice which our generation must necessarily make. Both Capitalism and Communism are products of the thinking and the practice of earlier times before the great modern revolutions in physics, in chemistry and in engineering had taken place. To suggest to peoples who must learn to live with atomic energy, with modern communications and with supersonic transport — to say nothing of the weapons of destruction which all these make possible — that they must first decide whether to be orthodox Communists or orthodox Capitalists is about as sensible as it would have been to tell the founders of the American Republic that they must first choose between the Ontological Argument and the Pope of Rome. The problem for our generation is not to take sides in an old, stale and more or less irrelevant quarrel, but to find and find quickly the new and unrealized means of living in a world never before inhabited by mankind.

The Marshall Plan, which puts life before orthodoxy, expresses an implicit American recognition of that fact. European and Asiatic recognition had been recorded long before. Communists aside, few Europeans or Asiatics regard Capitalism and Communism as the two alternatives of our time or the ideological struggle between them as an inevitable conflict. All of Europe which is free to do so has already moved in a political and economic direction which leads neither to one nor to the other, and the *masses* of the Chinese, if their views are truthfully reported to us, are heartily sick of both.

Moscow is no more the Rome, nor Communism the faith, of all those throughout the world who struggle for economic and social justice than New York is the Athens, and Capitalism the philosophy, of all those who believe in individual liberty and the rights of man. Organized labor, where it is not hounded by the police or driven by the mere compulsion of despair, looks anywhere but to Moscow. And as for the capital of freedom, there has never been a time since the American Revolution when fewer foreign believers in the cause of freedom hoped to find it here. American prestige among those who believe, or would like to believe, in the American cause is at its lowest point, and Russian prestige, among those who thought of the Russian Revolution as a revolution against imperialism or a revolution against the exploitation of oppressed peoples or a revolution against militarism and the secret police, has altogether collapsed. When men of free minds and honest opinions say what they really think these days in Europe and South America and the East, they curse both houses as bitterly as the dying Mercutio:

> They have made worms' meat of me: I have it!
> And soundly too: — your houses!

The truth is that the one explanation of the inevitability of conflict and of war is as unconvincing as the other. A future religious war is no more inevitable than a future imperialistic war. Not only has nothing yet *happened* which makes it necessary to believe in war: nothing is yet foreseeable which makes war inescapable or probable or even likely. It is not the facts of record or the facts in prospect which create the expectation of war: it is the expectation of war which gives the facts of record and the facts in prospect their tragic color.

But why then does the expectation exist? Why is our generation haunted as it is by the sense of disaster? Why have we lost the confidence in peace? It seems clear to me that that question cannot be answered either by a reading of diplomatic history or a study of political theory. The answer lies not outward in the world but inward in ourselves. Those who maintain that the crisis of our time is a moral crisis are precisely right. It is a moral crisis — but in the most personal and human sense: not in the institutional sense in which the phrase is commonly used. The problem is not one of restoring the authority of a code or establishing the discipline of a church. The problem is one of recovering the individual confidence and courage which men must bring to institutions: which institutions can never confer upon men.

Strong emotions — fears and hatreds — crystallize around the poles of the antagonism of Russia and the United States. But they crystallize not because the poles distill them but because the hatreds and the fears exist. It is not because Capitalism is Capitalism and Communism is Communism that men respond to the antagonism between them as they do, but because ours is a time of extreme personal insecurity and private frustration in which anything that touches the problems of individual responsibility or individual freedom produces reactions of a violent character. The mob emotions with regard to Communists and Communism exhibited from time to time in the United States, and the mob emotions with regard to Capitalism and Capitalists exhibited from time to time in Russia, are not affirmations of positive faith in Capitalism or Communism. They are confessions of insecurity and fear.

It is in this almost universal personal insecurity, not in the impersonal abstractions of politics and economics, that the true explanation of the anxiety and apprehensiveness of our time must be sought. Over the space of a very few generations, industrial and scientific developments, with their social and economic consequences, have produced a world so vast, so involved and so complicated as to be wholly unmanageable to individual human beings even in the small and intimate dimensions of the direction of their private lives. Events are removed from their causes and wrapped in remote confusion until they become as inhuman and as impersonal as fate.

Starvation or surfeit, sickness or health, life or death, are determined by forces over which no man has control. Great epidemics of depression sweep over the economic life, and the human life, of whole continents and even of the earth itself. Wars are precipitated without the motion, and without the knowledge, of the millions upon millions of human beings who will take part in them and whom they will destroy.

Individual action in individual defense against these huge disasters appears impossible. There seems to be no place to make a stand and nothing against which to strike — only shadows and abstractions: impalpable and imponderable things with which struggle is impossible. Everything a man touches seems to him impersonal, statistical, unmotivated, mechanical: even the thoughts in which he comes to think; even the works of public art by which he sees — a vast mechanical vocabulary of electrically animated images without smell or touch, of electrically vibrated words without mouths or breath. The most cruel and painful crimes become as impersonal and vast as the disasters of nature and no more to be condemned or judged. Men are murdered by millions and buried together in common graves and the photographs of their uncountable entangled bones are left us as the symbols of ourselves.

It is our experience of that impersonal and neuter world which explains the curious, nerveless fatality which afflicts our time. We believe that we have lost control of our destiny and we are willing therefore to believe that destiny is imposed upon us. We hate war and we desire peace but we no longer assume that the choice of war or peace is ours. Part of the world has made a virtue of this weakness, erecting the universal fatalism into a deterministic philosophy which carries mankind forward toward peace or toward war without election of its own. Part continues to talk in the vocabulary of a freedom which, because it has lost the corresponding responsibility by which freedom lives, becomes increasingly an abstraction. Those on the one side believe in the suicide of war because their philosophy predicts it. Those on the other believe in the suicide of war because they regard themselves as helpless to prevent it. And the consequence is that a war which none but madmen and bigots want — which not even bigots and madmen will survive — draws nearer day by day.

It is undoubtedly true that one cannot have peace merely by wishing for it. But it is even more true that one cannot have peace unless one wishes for it — and believes in the wish. Until we can escape, and unless we can escape, from the sense of helplessness and the even more murderous sense of necessity which, between them, have paralyzed our minds, the vast human majority of decent men and women who hate war will face war notwithstanding. It is in this sense that the problem of peace is a personal problem and a moral problem. Those in every city, in every town, in every house where peace is talked of, who say, What can I *do*, What can *I* do, have asked the only sensible question. Until that question is answered — until we have learned how individual human beings can recover a measure of control of the conditions of their lives in the world which science and technology have created — the will to peace will be merely a hope which will grow fainter with every tendentious speech and every diplomatic manoeuvre.

One of the wisest of living Americans, and certainly one of the most realistic, put the case in its simplest terms a few months ago. "The essential question," wrote Secretary Stimson on his eightieth birthday, "is one we should have to answer if there were not a Communist alive. Can we make freedom and prosperity real in the present world?" The essential question is not a question imposed by the existence of Communism or the opposition of Communism to Capitalism. It is not a question imposed by Russia or by the rivalry of Russia and the United States. It is a question imposed by the conditions of the world in which we live, and the relation to that world of individual men and women. We must make prosperity "real," which means to make life secure, in the changed and different world in which we live. And we must make freedom "real," which means to recover the sense of purpose and of will, the sense of fundamental human dignity, which the changed and different world has taken from us. Both are necessary to a peaceful world. Without the last, not even the will to peace can be assured.

1947

7

The Conquest of America

American foreign policy was a mirror image of Russian foreign policy: whatever the Russians did, we did in reverse . . . And the result was a declaration of political bankruptcy such as few great nations . . . have ever confessed to.

7

THE CONQUEST OF AMERICA

SOMETIME ALONG IN THE NINETEEN-EIGHTIES, when the world has left us as far behind as we have left the years that followed the First World War, somebody is going to publish a piece called *The Late Forties*. I hope to be dead at the time.

The subject of this piece will be the conquest of the United States by the Russians. It will begin more or less as follows:

Never in the history of the world was one people as completely dominated, intellectually and morally, by another as the people of the United States by the people of Russia in the four years from 1946 through 1949. American foreign policy was a mirror image of Russian foreign policy: whatever the Russians did, we did in reverse. American domestic politics were conducted under a kind of upside-down Russian veto: no man could be elected to public office unless he was on record as detesting the Russians, and no proposal could be carried, from a peace plan at one end to a military budget at the other, unless it could be demonstrated that the Russians wouldn't like it. American political controversy was controversy sung to the Russian tune; left-wing movements attacked right-wing movements not on American issues but on Russian issues, and right-wing movements replied with the same arguments turned round about. American education was Russian education backward: ignorance of Communism was the principal educational objective recognized by politicians and the general press, and the first qualification demanded of a teacher was that he should not be a Communist himself, should not have met persons who might have been Communists, and should never have read books which could tell him what Communism was. American intellectual life revolved around Russian intellectual life: writers stopped writing and convoked enormous meetings in expensive hotels to talk about Russia for days at a time, with the result that the problems of American culture (*if that self-conscious and over-fingered word is still in use in 1980*) became reflections of the problems of Russian culture. Even religious dogma was Russian dogma turned about: the first duty of a good Christian in the United States in those years was not to love his enemies but to hate the Communists — after which he was told to pray for them if he could.

All this, moreover — *so the article will continue* — all this took place not in a time of national weakness or decay but precisely at the moment when the United States, having engineered a tremendous triumph, and fought its way to a brilliant victory in the greatest of all wars, had reached the highest point of world power ever achieved by a single state. The American national income had doubled and doubled again in a generation. The American standard of living was far in advance of any other, including — including particularly — the Russian. The American industrial potential balanced, and over-balanced, that of the rest of the industrial world. American technological supremacy was so obvious that it was taken for granted, and American products were so far superior that they were used or copied everywhere on earth.

It was not, in other words, a weak and declining people, caught in the expanding shadow of history's new master,

which gave up its independent mind, contracted its national
will to the dry negation of the will of others and threw away
the historic initiative which, in the lives of nations as in the
lives of men, is the key to greatness. It was the most powerful
people in the world — a people still young in a continent still
new — a people which, only a generation before, had been
regarded as brash to the point of arrogance, cocksure to the
verge of folly and so wholly certain of its future and itself
that travelers wrote books about the national assurance. It
was the nation, in brief, which had been chiefly famous among
other nations because it conceived of its present not in terms
of its past but of its future — the nation which spoke with
a straight face and with entire sincerity of the American dream.

It ought to be possible for a good historian with a lively
sense of the ridiculous to amuse himself and his readers for
some pages with variations on that theme. But what will be
hardest for us to take — those of us who are left around —
will not be the ridicule of our successors but their sympathetic
understanding. For it is unlikely that any future account of
the prodigious paradox of our conduct will fail to reach the
conclusion that we lost our way as a people, and wandered
into the Russian looking-glass, primarily because we were
unable to think.

Neither our political leaders, the men of the eighties will
conclude, nor our Public Voices, nor the resounding apparatus
of radio and press in which minds were made up in our
epoch, seemed capable of understanding the nature of the
crisis in which we were caught or the role our position in the
world called on us to play. Instead we confused one of
several consequences of the crisis with the crisis itself, en-
larged upon a necessary police operation until it became not

only *a* national policy but *the* national policy, and roped ourselves as a sort of vast sea anchor, to the purposes and policies
of a rival state.

As to the nature of the crisis, it will be noted that the general opinion held among us, however individuals might dissent,
was the opinion that the troubles of our age were international
in character; that they had been precipitated by the rise of
Communism; that Communism was a great new revolutionary
force; that the way to resolve the crisis, therefore, was to resist
and contain and presumably strangle the Communist revolution. As to the role we were called upon to play, we were apparently convinced that the United States, being the most
powerful nation in the world, must bear the burden of the
labor of resistance and containment; that this labor, being difficult and dangerous, must take precedence over everything
else inside the country or out — particularly inside; and that
all purely American objectives and purposes, including the
realization of the great traditional objectives of American
life, must not only be subordinated to the accomplishment of
the task of containment but even, in certain cases, sacrificed
to it.

The paradoxical conclusion to which we brought ourselves,
in other words, was based on equally paradoxical arguments
derived from what will seem to our successors a wholly aston-
ishing assumption. For it will be obvious to men who examine
our times in historical perspective that the crisis in which we
were caught was not at all what we thought it, that it was not
new but had been produced by the cumulative changes of
many centuries; that it was not a crisis in international rela-
tions but a crisis in civilization, a crisis in culture, a crisis in
the condition of man; that it had not been precipitated by the
rise of Communism, which was, indeed, one of its consequences, or by a conspiracy in the Kremlin, which was one of

its incidents, but by a tragic lag between the disintegration of
one order of society — the petering out of one historical era —
and the flowering of another; that Communism was not a
new revolutionary force but one of several forms of authoritarian reaction, political, philosophical and clerical, organized
in terms of the disintegrating order of society and competing
with each other for the domination of that disappearing
world; that the true revolutionary force in our epoch — the
force moving not backward toward the disintegrating world
but forward toward the world which had not yet been created
— was the force which had been released at the end of the
eighteenth century and the beginning of the nineteenth by
the words and actions of a few men, most of them Americans;
that the belief that the world crisis could be resolved merely
by resisting and containing Communism was, therefore, a
delusive belief, and the conclusion that the realization of
the historic American purpose must be deferred and subordinated to the defeat of the Russian purpose was a false conclusion
from every point of view — political, intellectual and moral.

We will hardly be in a position — those of us who live
that long — to refute this indictment. No one but the
ignorant man or the fanatic believes even now that Communism is really the origin of our ills or that the world suffers
solely from the attentions of personal devils — Stalin from
our point of view: Truman from the Russian. We know perfectly well, whatever we may read in the general run of our
newspapers or hear from the noisier commentators on the
air, that the real difficulty of our time goes deeper than
Russian imperialism or Communist fraud. The real difficulty
touches life itself, not merely the manipulation of life. It
involves a conflict not between nations but between worlds:
a dying world not altogether dead; a new world conceived

but not yet born. The dying world is the world which reached its highest European integration in the Middle Ages: the world in which men were able to realize themselves and fulfill their lives as members of the closely knit body of a city or a church or a state or a feudal or institutional structure of some kind. This world began to decay with the Renaissance and has disintegrated with a rapidly accelerated momentum over the years which include the two great world wars. The new world is the world in which men, exiled from an institutional security and an institutional fulfillment, will realize themselves as individual human beings answerable to their consciences and God. The new world, though it was foreseen and its possibility declared a hundred and seventy years ago, has yet to be established. The limbo in which we live is the interval between the two.

The theory, propounded by the Communists and their authoritarian rivals, that Communism is a revolutionary force, will not stand up. A revolutionary force, as distinguished from a reactionary force, is one which moves not backward against the flow of change but forward with it. It is a force which dares to take the revolutionary risk of trusting the flowering of the tree, the meandering of the current. The whole movement of human life, violently accelerated over the last few centuries, has been a movement toward the separation of the individual consciousness from the common consciousness, the common sleep, the animal sleep — a movement toward the differentiation of the individual from the community of the tribe, and, before that, from the community of the "natural" life of universal instinct. Communism is not a force which moves with that current. On the contrary, Communism, like the rest of its authoritarian rivals, seeks to cure the sickness of the condition of man by turning back against the current of human evolution to that decaying city of hierarchical and disciplined order in which mankind, at certain sacrifices of manhood, may find seclusion and retreat.

The one force which can claim the revolutionary title in the world we live in, the one force which can claim to move in the direction of life, is the force that Jefferson put into words. Later Americans have, it is true, betrayed it, both in terms and actions. Its vocabulary has been appropriated again and again for private advantage. Its victories have been corrupted by hypocrisy and cynicism and selfishness. Its articles of faith have been made the catechism of a faithless materialism. Its hero, the individual human being, grown cancerous with greed, has swollen on occasion to the morbid and malignant figure of irresponsible and grasping power — the "rugged individual" whom some still think of as American. But though the hope has been betrayed and forgotten in one generation and another, the living seed remains: the seed remains and grows. It is this seed, this influence, this force, this force of revolution, which is the living thing in the Republic. Without it, the Unted States is so much land, so many people, such and such an accumulation of wealth. With it the United States is a stage upon the journey of mankind.

But it is not only because we were wrong and fainthearted in our thinking that we will be blamed by those who come after us. It is not only because we had no reason to subordinate our own purposes to the defeat of Russian purposes and thus to surrender to Russia the initiative we had always held before. We will be blamed also because the negative and defensive attitude of mind to which we committed the Republic was mistaken and mischievous and evil in itself. It was mistaken because it was incapable of achieving even its own negative purpose. It was mischievous because it choked up the deep springs of the moral life of the nation. It was evil because it deprived the world of the thing the world most needed — a positive and believable alternative to the grim choice the authoritarians held before mankind.

The inadequacy of the position we took, even within its own narrow and negative purpose, is only too obvious. Neither Communism nor any other body of positive belief can be overcome in a period of world-wide dissatisfaction and unrest merely by denying it, or by offering, as a substitute, the world of things as they are. It can be fought only by facing it with a true alternative. And the true alternative to Communism is not the world of things as they are, nor, even more certainly, is it some kind of authoritarianism. The real choice is the choice between all forms of authoritarianism on the one side and, on the other, the dream of a whole and responsible human freedom. The real conflict, in other words, the underlying conflict, is not the struggle between the Kremlin and the West which the press associations report from day to day. The real conflict is the conflict between world reaction, which preaches submission to authority, whether of a state or a man or a party or a church, and world revolution which is still, however the various reactionaries may attempt to confuse the issue, the revolution of the individual, the revolution of the whole man.

Stated in terms of structure, the real alternatives are, at the one pole, a cellular, authoritarian society in which individual human beings may live their lives through the life of the society as a whole, and at the other, a world of individual men, whose relation to each other, in the freedom of their individuality, will create a society in which each can live as himself.

For the United States, in such a situation, to adopt a wholly negative policy aimed at the containment of Communism, is not only to fail in the effort to defeat Communism, but to miss the real American objective as well; and, worse still, to obstruct one form of authoritarian reaction to the advantage of others. Having unwisely elected to forgo our own purposes as a people, and to resist the purposes of the Russians, we have found ourselves, not once but many times in the past four years, supporting those who hate the revolution of the individual as violently as the Communists hate it. And not only abroad but here at home. For, by putting the hatred and fear of Russia first we have opened the sacred center of our lives — our most essential freedoms, the freedoms of mind and thought — to those among us who have always hated those freedoms and who know well how to use our fear of Russia as a screen to cover their attacks. The spread of legalized thought control from points of infection in the Congress to legislature after legislature across the country is not the work of chance. It is the work of freedom-hating men. And we have laid the city open to them by our fears.

The second vice of the morbid and negative national opinion we have accepted in these years — its mischievous influence on our spiritual life — may be judged by other evidence, no less obvious to those who wish to see it. The soul of a people is the image it cherishes of itself, the aspect in which it sees itself against the past, the attributes to which its future conduct must respond. To destroy that image is to destroy, in a very real sense, the identity of the nation, for to destroy the image is to destroy the means by which the nation recognizes what it is and what it has to do. But the image a people holds of itself is created not by words alone or myths but by its actions. Unless the actions are appropriate to the image, the image is blurred. If the actions deny the image, the image is destroyed.

What is happening in the United States under the impact of the negative and defensive and often frightened opinion of these years is the falsification of the image the American

people have long cherished of themselves as beginners and
begetters, changers and challengers, creators and accomplish-
ers. A people who have thought of themselves for a hundred
and fifty years as having purposes of their own for the
changing of the world cannot learn overnight to think of
themselves as the resisters of another's purposes without
beginning to wonder who they are. A people who have been
real to themselves because they were *for* something cannot
continue to be real to themselves when they find they are
merely *against* something. They begin to ask questions. Who,
then, are they? Are they still the journeying restless nation
to which the future was a direction on a map and the duty of
the son was to turn his back on his father's gateposts, or
have they turned around and headed the other way? Are
they still the new nation of discoverers and inventors who
were never satisfied to leave things as they were but remade
the world in every generation, or are they an old nation
now of protectors and preservers whose character it is to
keep things as they used to be? Are they still the young
champions of freedom in the west who warned the Holy
Alliance to let the fires of revolutionary freedom burn as
they might on this continent, or have they joined with those
who put the fires out?

The old words of freedom and revolution are still around,
louder than ever, but somehow they are not the same. Revolution, which was once a word spoken with pride by every
American who had the right to claim it, has become a word
spoken with timidity and doubt and even fear. And freedom which, in the old days, was something you *used* has
now become something you *save* — something you put away
and protect like your other possessions, like a deed or a bond
in a bank. The true test of freedom is in its *use*. It has no
other test. But freedom in this sick and melancholy time of

ours has become, not a thing to use, but a thing to defend. Even the word American has changed. The American once was a man bound to his country and his fellows by a common belief in something not yet realized that he loved. Now he is a man — or there are those who tell him he is a man — bound to his country and the rest by a common hatred of something looming that he fears.

What has been happening to the people of the United States in the last few years is something that can destroy the inward vitality of the nation if we let it go on. It is possible for writers of a certain journalistic mentality to look at the change and rejoice in it as proof that we have grown up as a country, that we have faced the harsh realities of life at last and that we have now become a great power. But a people which recognizes its unity only in its opposition to another people, which understands its purposes only in its resistance to another purpose, is not a people which has a unity or a purpose of its own. And it is not a great people whatever its power or its wealth. The great nations in the history of the world have been the nations which proposed, the nations which asserted, the nations which conceived. The United States was such a nation when it knew its mind and declared its belief and acted to create the world it wanted.

From the American point of view, then, the severest indictment of this generation of men and women will be the charge that we falsified the American image and thus undermined the spiritual integrity of the nation. But there will be other accusations from other quarters and some of them will be even harsher than our own. There will be the judgment of the men of conscience and concern and honest mind in every country who, when all the arguments are in, write down the verdicts. And what they will say of us will certainly be this: that we had it in our power at a critical moment in history when the whole future of humanity hung in balance to present a true and hopeful alternative to the iron choice with which the world was faced and that we did not do it; that we did not do it even though the true alternative was the course to which our whole past and our entire tradition had committed us; that instead of doing it we built a wall against one half the evil but not the other, and made the wall still higher by tearing down for its construction some of the dearest of our own beliefs.

It will be difficult for us to answer that charge in whatever tribunal of the future such verdicts are debated. We can argue with great conviction that we had no choice, in the face of Russian threats of force and Russian conspiracies of fraud, but to arm ourselves and to resist. And it is true that we had no choice. But it is true also — and no one who remembers what has been said in the American press in these days, and in the American Senate, can deny that it is true — that our policy in this situation was not merely to put ourselves in a position to resist and then go on about our American purpose: on the contrary our purpose and our policy *became* resistance. Resistance to the Russians became an end and object in itself. And the result was a declaration of political bankruptcy such as few great nations in the course of history have ever confessed to. When Senators, urging recognition and aid to Franco, argued that that enemy of everything this Republic is or has ever stood for, deserved our friendship because he had fought the Communists and Russia, they said in effect that what we believe in is nothing, but what we hate is the gateway to our minds. No one in his senses denies that Russian fraud, Russian lies, Russian militarism, Russian imperialism, Russian stupidity and fanaticism and greed left us no choice but to rearm. But no one in his senses can deny either that we made of this necessity the excuse for a failure to achieve a policy of our own. That failure may well turn out to have been the costliest blunder in our history.

What needed to be done in the years immediately following the second war is obvious even now. What needed to be done both for the purposes of peace and for the hope of human life was to break the impotent and issueless deadlock, the total spiritual impasse, between the two authoritarianisms of right and left by declaring, as alternative to them both, a free man's solution to the problems of this time. To the shrill bat voices of those who cry out on this foreshore of history from the direction of Franco's Spain on the one side and Stalin's Moscow on the other that the world has no choice but to choose between them, and that peace between them is impossible — to these shrill and cynical and brutal voices there should have been a man's voice answering, like Ulysses' above Hell's offering of blood, to tell them both they lied.

The answer to the inevitable choice between the two authoritarianisms with their heartless promise of a bigoted and bloody war is the voice of a single man shouting that there is no such necessity, that there is a road ahead not backward, a man's road: one man's road. What was needed was to raise this voice. What was needed was to declare, with the full and reasoned conviction of a great people behind the declaration, that there was still a man's way out of the wreck of our disasters; that the revolution of the individual, far from being finished, had not yet begun; that the words of that revolution were not merely words but meanings also; that the meanings could be given and could be understood. What was needed was a re-declaration of the revolution of the individual, in terms applicable to the conditions which now exist in the world and with a full and realistic recognition of the difficulties they present: a re-assessment of the problem and a reaffirmation of the hope. Only one nation in the world was capable of that act and the nation was our own. And we did nothing. We built walls.

It will not be possible for us to argue, when that charge is made against us, that we did not see what needed to be done. Neither will it be possible for us to plead that there was nothing we could do — nothing we could do as a people: that a people cannot think itself through problems such as these: that the labor of redefining, of implementing, the revolution of the individual in a modern industrial society is a labor of such difficulty that only the technicians of industry and politics can accomplish it: that to ask an entire nation, by an act of choice, an act of will, to make freedom a reality under the conditions of contemporary life is to talk in rhetoric, not reason. It is true of course that the labor is difficult; nothing more so. It is true that it will require much technical skill, political, industrial, mechanical and economic. But it is not true that it is the technical difficulty that stands in the way. What really stands in the way is the moral difficulty, the difficulty of choice, the difficulty which only the people, acting as a people, can remove.

No intelligent man believes the technical difficulties are insurmountable — and least of all in a country of great natural wealth, a high level of administrative and technological intelligence and large reserves of skilled labor. If the people of such a country were determined to hammer out a political and industrial and economic order in which individual men — all men as individuals — should be capable of living and working in dignity and freedom and self-respect with an adequate opportunity for a realization of their full potentialities as human beings, the thing could be done. It makes a great deal of difference, as Bishop Berkeley observed, whether you put truth in the first place or in the second. It makes a great deal of difference whether you say that your objective is a free society but that you wish first to be prosperous, or first to be comfortable or first to be something else, or whether you say that your objective *is a free society*.

Certainly the political problems, difficult and delicate though they may be, are not insoluble. Some, like the control or the liquidation of monopolies which stand in the way of individual initiative, have a long history in this country. Others, like the struggle to liberate individuals from the degrading fear of unemployment or old age or sickness are less familiar — at least in the United States. Still others, like the over-riding question of the relation between individual freedom and the intervention of the state, have a meaning for our generation which they did not have for generations before. But only a man who did not wish to find an answer to questions such as these would argue that no answer can be found.

And what is true of the technical difficulties in the political area is true also of the technical difficulties in the economic field and even in the industrial. If the individual human being became the object of primary concern, rather than the manufactured product or its marketing, progress would be made which now is thought impossible. If, for example, one-tenth of the energy now devoted to the development of gadgets no one ever needed until an advertisement told him he could not live without them, were devoted to the development of new industrial methods which would permit a man to work as a man instead of working as an adjunct to a machine, even that greatest of human emancipations might be accomplished.

No, it is not the technical problem requiring special knowledge and unusual skill which stands in the way of the great alternative of freedom. It is not the failure of the engineers or the economists or the political philosophers to devise the new form of a free society which has robbed us of our initia-

tive as a people. We cannot excuse or justify ourselves by
complaining that no one has told us what to do. The real
obstacle is the obstacle of ends, not means. The real obstacle
is the obstacle of will, not method. Those who follow us and
observe our failures will say we did not wish sufficiently for
freedom. And they will be right.

Freedom—individual freedom—was always a hard choice.
With us it has become a choice which many men — many of
the most intelligent and sensitive among us — find it impossible to make. When the revolution of the individual was
first declared the choice of freedom meant the choice of
struggle against the established order of the state and church.
With us, in a world in which the old established order, weakened by the earthquakes of four centuries, has all but collapsed,
leaving mankind in a roofless city without interpreters or
guardians but alone, the choice of freedom has become the
choice of going on, each for himself, across the ruin and the
rubble to that unknown future city men will build as men.

When the revolution of the individual was first declared, it
was declared against the masters of the world, and armies
fought it. To continue it now is to continue it not by armies
but by single men, and not by battles against the former masters of the world but by lonely conquests of responsibility
and freedom. There is no harder choice than the choice of
singleness and duty in a broken world, and it is not remarkable perhaps that many of those of our generation who
should have been champions of the revolution of the individual — poets, writers, men whose first necessity is freedom
— have been unable to accept the burden: have turned back
instead to one or the other of the authoritarianisms where they
can stretch the painted canvas tent of dogma between them
and the empty sky where once the roofs were. But though it
is possible to understand why many of the best have left us,

and why great numbers of the American people have given up the lonely pursuit of liberty for the safer assurance of discipline and peace, it is not possible for that reason to forgive their desertion, or to justify it, or to forget that it is through them and their default that the world has lost the great and positive affirmation it so desperately needed.

If we ask ourselves where we are now, we are precisely there. We are at that point in our moral history as a people at which we have failed, for the first time in a moment of decision, to assert our moral purpose. We have not yet denied that purpose — the cock has not crowed for the last time — but we have failed to assert it. We have not yet changed the direction of our national life but we have lost our momentum, we have lost our initiative. We have not yet rejected our role as a revolutionary people moving with the great revolutionary current of history but we have ceased to move, we have begun to resist, to oppose. It does not require a prophet to see that we have come to a moment of critical decision — a decision which is none the less critical because it may be taken un-aware. If we do nothing, if we continue to stand where the 'forties have left us, we will have taken one decision, we will have ceased to be what we were and we will inevitably become something else, something very different, something the found-ers of the republic would not recognize and surely would not love. Only by action, only by moral action, only by moral action at the highest level — only by affirmative recommitment to the revolution of the individual which was the vital and creative impulse of our national life at the beginning of our history — only by these means can we regain ourselves.

1949

8

The Revulsion of Decency

What has happened . . . when the figure American history most detests, the figure of the self-confessed informer . . . can be spoken of with praise?

8

THE REVULSION OF DECENCY

OUR COUNTRY IS JUST NOW RECOVERING from the most protracted moral and intellectual binge in the history of the Republic, and troubled citizens from one coast to the other are asking themselves, in revulsion and anxiety and disgust, a question which none of us can decently ignore.

They are asking themselves: What happened to this nation? What came over us? How could we, we particularly, we of all the peoples of the earth, we who have always boasted of our courage and our confidence and our belief in ourselves, our respect for each other, our trust in our own people, our faith in our institutions of self-government — how could *we* fall from ourselves so far? And into such morbid and unmanly fears? Into such spiteful hatreds? Such hysterical suspicion of each other and ourselves? Such neurotic terror of the machinations of our enemies? Such cowardly distrust of our own destiny? Such ignorant forgetfulness of the great meaning of our past?

These are not rhetorical questions. They are real questions. They ring with iron tongues in the minds of responsible men and women of all opinions and all parties. They produce examinations of conscience among United States Senators of the opposition as well as hours of sleepless anxiety among officers of government. They echo in the questions and answers, the arguments and the responses of citizens everywhere. And they will not be silenced.

The facts, the ostensible facts to which they relate, do not silence them. There is no single fact or combination of facts which explains what has happened. There is no devil in the piece, though there are villains enough — no devil, that is, of sufficient stature and influence to have shaken and undermined the morale of a great people, the most powerful nation now on earth. The ostensible facts are these:

A minor politician without moral authority in his own state or anywhere else, speaking on a purely political occasion to a wholly political audience, alleged that there were two hundred and five Communists in the Department of State of the United States. This unsupported allegation was picked up by the press. A Senate committee was appointed to investigate. The two hundred and five became variously eighty-one and fifty-seven. The eighty-one or fifty-seven became a dozen or so actual names. The dozen or so actual names proved to belong to people who had already been investigated by the FBI and cleared by loyalty boards and committees of the previous Congress which the opposition controlled. The dozen or so actual names were then replaced in the news by a single alleged chief Communist and master spy on whose guilt or innocence the whole case was to stand or fall — as though charges of treason, in a country like the United States, were no more than bets in poker: doubles or quits. The single alleged chief Communist and master spy turned out not to be in the State Department at all, and to be anything but a meek and willing victim into the bargain. The charge of "master spy" was then withdrawn. Evidence was offered. The evidence proved to be rumor and private opinion presented for the most part by persons who admitted they had been Communists once themselves but claimed now to have left the party.

Nothing in the entire factual record, in other words, was definite or certain or beyond question but one thing: that charges of Communism in the Department of State had been made involving something between two hundred and five persons and one, and that the conduct of the politician making these charges had not been such as to inspire confidence in the entire singleness of his desire to get at the truth. And nevertheless these vague and fluctuating charges, and the hearings in connection with them, and the evidence offered or not offered in their support, have obsessed the minds of a great part of the American people, pre-empted the time of the officers of their government, divided the Congress as the Congress has not been divided since the Civil War and weakened the country in the face, not only of its enemies, but of those it needs as friends.

Small wonder that decent citizens, looking back over such a record in the light of returning common sense, should ask themselves what has happened to their country. If there is no factual explanation of the national obsession what then was the cause? The press, which so many of us blame for so many ills? The irresponsibility of certain publishers and the greed of others? The grating voices of political partisans, disguised as commentators, on the air? I do not think so. Radio and press, though they may exploit a national state of mind to their own profit rather than to the advantage of the public interest, do not themselves create the mental climate of the United States. The practices of certain columnists who have made a profitable business of the sale of hate and calumny over the past ten years may have provided the politicians engaged in this particular campaign with their precedents and models, but the press as a whole can hardly be held responsible for anything but the initial inflation of an unsupported allegation into a ballooning newspaper story.

Where then does the responsibility lie? Quite clearly, I think, in the one place where most of us are least likely to look for it — in ourselves. Ten years ago a political speech like the speech which set off this chain reaction in the deterioration of American morale would not have been noticed outside the Hearst or the McCormick industries. This year it is published on the front page of responsible newspapers. And why is it published there? A curious editorial in *The New York Times* provides the probable answer.

Deploring the effect on national morale of the publication of unsubstantiated charges of disloyalty in government departments, the editors of that distinguished journal proposed, as others have proposed since, that a national committee be appointed to investigate — the *Times'* nominees being Messrs. Baruch, Eisenhower and Hoover. Why so important a committee should be set up to investigate the *lack* of evidence to support charges which no patriotic or honorable man would make unless he *had* evidence, the editors of the *Times* did not explain. Neither did they state why a great and responsible newspaper which believed that charges it was publishing were of doubtful truth, and that the publication of these charges was a public disservice, should go on publishing them on its front page. The concern of the editors of the *Times* was with something else — something deeper and more troublesome than one man's recklessness or another man's responsibility. Their concern was with the national state of mind. What they were saying in effect was this: that in the present state of mind of the American people even the greatest of their newspapers had lost control of its essential function, and that it is the national state of mind, rather than the conduct of a particular politician, which should occupy our thoughts.

Whatever one may think of the logic of the argument, there can be little doubt of the soundness of the underlying assumption. It is not because the American press published defamatory rumors as front-page news that faith in the great American conviction of the dignity and worth of the individual human being has been shaken in the United States. It is because faith in the dignity and worth of the individual human being has been shaken that defamatory rumors could be published as front-page news without meeting the general public indignation which would have silenced them in a braver time. It is not because a frightened and apparently shameless politician attempted to terrify us with fluctuating statistics of disloyalty in our government and hysterical forecasts of the imminent Communization of the United States that we have lost the confidence and courage which characterized our people in the past. It is because courage and confidence have drained away that a man of such dubious qualifications, ignorant of our national character and unfamiliar with our tradition, could persuade us to listen to his panic talk.

The real question, the question every decent citizen of this country must ask himself in all earnestness of heart and mind and conscience, is the question: What has brought our convictions and beliefs to this low state? What has happened to a tradition of self-reliance, of mutual respect, of confidence in each other, of belief in the people and their capacity to govern themselves, of faith in the institutions through which their self-government operates? What has happened to a tradition which goes back for centuries on this continent? What has happened to that tradition when a campaign of innuendo and suspicion and distrust, wholly alien to our history, can thrive among us? What has happened to that tradition when the author of these doubts, the perpetrator of schism, the agent of fear, can be made a kind of public hero by audiences which regard themselves as American? What has happened to that tradition when the figure American history most detests, the figure of the self-confessed informer, engaged in his divisive and subversive business, can be spoken of with praise?

That is the real question. That is the question which must give every American, whatever his party or his economic position or his race or his church, long anxious hours. For it is, without any qualification whatever, the most serious question history has asked us since the American Civil War. If the belief of the American people in themselves and in each other has truly declined to such a point that cynically unsubstantiated charges, and naked rumors, and hearsay suspicions, can throw our national life, at any moment and under any circumstances, into such an uproar as we have witnessed in shame and disgust these last long weeks, then the Republic is not only in danger: it is in greater danger than it has faced since the War Between the States. And what it is in danger of is something far more deadly than Communist armies without or Communist conspiracy within, deadly as these things are. What it is in danger of is the loss of its own soul.

I for my part do not believe that the faith of the American people in themselves and in each other has been corrupted to this point. I am comforted, as we have all been comforted, by the great and growing wave of indignation and revulsion against this strategy of fear. The American conscience has spoken, without regard to politics or party, in the words of one of the great moral leaders of the Republic, the former Secretary of War and State, Henry L. Stimson. It has spoken in the voice of Senator Margaret Chase Smith and those who associated themselves with her noble protest on the Senate floor. A minority in this country which was apparently ignorant of the American tradition, and uninstructed in the American past, has had a lesson which may stand both it and the Republic in good stead. It has learned that neither political ambition masquerading as public service, nor bigotry disguised as patriotism, will long deceive the people of this country if the fundamental American belief — the belief in the dignity and worth of the human individual — is challenged.

But though the country is rapidly recovering its self-respect, strengthened in its devotion to common decency and common right, the underlying question still remains and still demands our answer. Unless we can understand why we were vulnerable to an attack upon our confidence and our courage on this occasion, we cannot be certain that, attacked again, we shall be stronger than we were.

It is my contention that the key to that essential understanding is to be found in the general position we have adopted with regard to the world crisis in which we live. Faced with the consequences, in human restlessness and discontent and desperation, of two world wars, and of an expanding industrial and technical revolution which has now reached to the farthest corners of Asia, we elected, at a critical moment in history, to resist the Communist exploitation of that situation rather than to act upon it affirmatively in the interest of our own belief in individual freedom. We chose the policy of the containment of Russia rather than the policy of the realization of the American dream. We turned our backs on those who talked about decent living standards for the peoples of Asia and Africa and committed ourselves instead to the men who proposed to encircle Communism with a ring of steel. We elected a destiny of permanent negation in place of the destiny of endless affirmation which had created our nation and our history as a people.

The effect of that decision on our fortunes abroad is obvious enough and has been recognized for what it is. Opinions differ as to the wisdom or lack of wisdom of our foreign policy but no one doubts that our present situation is a result, in one sense or another, of the decision to resist. What we have not recognized — or had not recognized until we found ourselves infected by the hysteria of these last few weeks — is the fact that the same decision has had consequences at home. And yet those consequences at home are even more obvious, and may be far more serious, than the consequences abroad. They have already produced the most dangerous corruption of fundamental decencies and beliefs which living Americans have seen on American soil. They are capable of bringing about a moral and political and religious revolution which would destroy the civilization which has been in process of formation on this continent from the Mayflower Compact through the Declaration of Independence, from the American Constitution to the latest legislative expression of the faith in human freedom.

If you impose upon a virile and creative people whose past history has been a history of the pursuit of their own purposes, the accomplishment of their own labors, the realization of their own hopes — if you impose upon such a people a doctrine not of achievement but of defense, not of the pursuit of their own ends but of the frustration of the ends of others — you create inevitably a psychological vacuum. And a psychological vacuum, like a vacuum anywhere else, will fill itself if it can. The American vacuum is no exception. It has filled itself. It filled itself first with an infatuated preoccupation with the very thing it had been created to exclude. Communism became the dominant obsession of the American mind, and every new attempt to hunt it out by Klieg lights, television and Congressional dramatics only enhanced its importance. A contemptible party, which had never been able to interest a minute fraction of the American people until blundering assailants in Congress and in state legislatures came to its assistance, was built up into an infernally powerful, diabolically intelligent and unbelievably efficient organization about which every reader of newspapers, every listener to radio, was daily informed. Theories of the subordination of the individual to the state, which had been detestable to American opinion from the foundation of the Republic and which the Communist Party had never been able to propagate here, were propagated for it by individuals and groups in Congress and out, who advocated restrictions on the fundamental American right to think as you please and say as you think, on the ground that it is more important to catch Communists than to *be* Americans. Even the idea of freedom itself was hacked down, by an infatuated logic, to fit the Communist obsession. A former Ambassador to Russia protested not long ago against the engraving of the Four Freedoms on a memorial because, he said, freedom from want and freedom from fear are Russian freedoms.

To contract the American dream because it might overlap the Russian propaganda was as remarkable a proof of preoccupation with Communism as a man could expect to see in a once courageous country. But there was worse to come. There was the momentary failure of American morale under the campaign of suspicion and fear of the past several months. And beyond that shameful incident — beyond it but shadowed in its murk — there was and is a further and a greater danger. There is the danger that the vacuum which has filled itself with a preoccupation with Communism, and which has carried that preoccupation to the point of a temporary loss of confidence in our own institutions under the mere breath of rumor and suspicion, will end by drawing into itself some

counter-Communism which we will accept, because it is coun-
ter-Communist, only to learn too late that it is counter-
American as well.

If you determine your national course of action by hostility
to Communism, and if you let your own traditional aspirations
for the creation of *your* kind of world wilt and wither, and
if, in the state of frustration and futility which must inevitably
follow, you permit Communist fraud and Russian threats and
Soviet duplicity to frighten you into a state of apprehension
and funk, you are very apt to turn for strength, not to your
own proven historical resources of self-reliance and individual
initiative and personal courage, but to some rival authoritarianism which, you believe, can defend you better than a purely
democratic, self-governing people can defend themselves.

It is not likely, I will be told, that a nation which has just
fought and won a terrible and costly war against one brand of
authoritarianism should turn to another to escape a third. And
I agree that it is not likely. I agree that it is not likely in spite of
the reckless and irresponsible things that have been said by certain Americans about that war since it was won. I agree that
it is not likely in spite of the foolish and fatuous things that
are still being said by certain Americans about anti-Communist
dictatorships in other countries. But no responsible American
citizen, face to face with the events of the past several months,
can contemplate the future with complacency even so. As
long as we continue in a state of mind which makes Communism, in mirror image, the dominant and controlling influence in our national life — a state of mind which leads
us to act from fear instead of hope — to act *against* instead
of *for* — as long as we continue in this state of mind, we
arm our demagogues and our ambitious men with terrible
weapons. As we have just now seen. Not until we have recovered our sense of ourselves, not until we have returned to

our traditional business of creating and building, not until
we can look at our time with eyes of purpose instead of eyes
of fear, will we be safe from enemies who, because they hate
the things we hate, we think of now as friends.

Many of us in the United States talk of the need for religion
in this critical time. To some what is required is the moral
rearmament of mankind for a struggle against amorality. To
others, the need is for a rededication to Christ in the battle
against anti-Christ. To still others our salvation lies in the
renunciation of the materialism which degrades our civilization, and the conversion of the world to spiritual things. These
are elevated aspirations and some of them are nobly held.
There is, however, another and a humbler labor which falls
not upon the churches but upon the schools and above all upon
those institutions of higher learning which must be responsible,
in our society, for the vitality of the concepts which have
shaped our thought.

What is essential to our escape from the trap of fear and
hate and worse in which we lie suffocating today is *a recovery
of a sense of purpose*. Without the passion of purpose no
nation however rich — no man or woman however talented —
can escape the evil things that breed in the dead air, and poison
and destroy.

But purpose is not merely a matter of a declaration of positive aims by your State Department — a new policy, foreign
or domestic. Purpose is not merely a question of what you
mean to do next. Purpose is a question also of *why you mean
to do it*. To what end? To accomplish what of human value?

When we in the United States were a nation of purpose, at
the full expression of our purpose as a nation, there was no
American who could not have answered either question without so much as pausing to draw breath. What we aimed to
do next was to open this continent to mankind to live in.

And the reason why we aimed to open this continent to mankind to live in was to create here a nation in which men could be free *as individuals* — think as they pleased and say as they thought and live the way men *should* live: in self-respect and confidence and courage. We meant to show the world that such a nation *could* be created — that men *could* live so — live like men.

In theory that is still our reason for existence. But it is a reason which survives today rather in our rhetoric than in our wills. And it is precisely there, or so it seems to me, that the men and women, students and teachers, of American colleges and universities, have a labor to perform. For the weakening of our wills in this regard — the weakening of our belief in the absolute value of the freedom and independence of the individual human mind — is a consequence not only of a change in ourselves but of a change in our world. It is, to put it bluntly, far more difficult to believe in the absolute worth and dignity of the human individual in the world we live in than in the world Thomas Jefferson lived in. But — and for the same reason — it is far more necessary also.

The belief in man — man as an individual — man as an individual free to think as he pleases and say as he thinks — man as an individual answerable only to his conscience and his God — this belief is not easy to articulate in realistic and self-evident terms in an industrialized society, in which men live in universal dependence on each other — it is not easy to state in terms of a neutral universe such as the universe modern physics has revealed to us. And yet, without a new and convincing articulation of belief in the unqualified right of the individual human being to think as he pleases and say what he thinks, regardless of the preconceptions and the creeds, the opinions and the prejudices, of governments or parties or organizations or churches, civilization as we have known it — civilization ennobled by science and crowned by art — civilization carried forward by the creative spirit and the enquiring mind — would be unthinkable. It would disappear behind the blank conformist institutionalism which, not only in Russia, not only in Europe, threatens to board up the outward windows of the world.

The colleges and universities of a free society are first — or should be first — among the defenders of a civilization in which freedom can survive. They have a duty, recognized by almost all of them, to resist the encroachments of bigotry and ignorance and prejudice and fear, upon their own — their academic — liberties: for without these liberties they are not schools at all but prisons of men's minds. They have, however, another duty also: to redefine and make articulate the underlying faith of freedom in itself: to light once more the guttering candle of man's reliance on himself in such a world as ours.

It is an inconceivably difficult labor, but one the universities and colleges alone can do. And it is well worth doing. Without the belief in man — the live and passionate belief in man — democracy is a rhetorical formula which will collapse whenever fear assaults it: which any demagogue can undermine. *With* the belief in man, democracy becomes the most powerful social structure in the world, because it is then the only social structure which is not only *structure* but moral force as well.

1950

9

The Sense of American Purpose

The real change as always is neither in our stars nor in our enemies but in ourselves.

9

THE SENSE OF AMERICAN PURPOSE

SIX YEARS AGO in the month of January, the United States was the greatest power in the world: materially speaking, the greatest power the world had ever seen. Six years ago whatever the fortunes of the war on either front, men were joined in a common determination which they recognized and which expressed itself in action. They were allied with peoples elsewhere in a common cause which had not only military victory, but lasting peace, as end and aim. They believed in themselves and in the future.

Today they believe, it seems, in neither. Today, their victory scarcely won, the American people are being told by officials in Washington and journalists everywhere that they face a new world war, not, this time, for the achievement of a purpose of their own but for the naked right to go on living — to survive. They are being told this and they listen. Bewildered and angry though they may be, they are listening. And listening, they are coming to believe. And why?

The answer, if you read the run of the American press, is Russia. A nation which was our ally in the war, a nation which our productivity and the intervention of our arms saved from disaster, has, since the war's end, turned upon us, violated her commitments to us, poisoned the minds of nations and of continents against us, and openly confessed a purpose to destroy us if she can.

It is true that Russia has done all this. One would have to go back to the history of the petty princelings of the Quattrocento to find a parallel to the duplicity, the cynicism, the brutality, the pompous arrogance of the rulers of the Russian people. But all this, much as it is, is still no answer to the question. Russia was a Communist country in 1945, committed to the Communist dogma of the inevitability of the collapse of such an economy as ours. She was also a populous country with enormous armies in the field. And yet we did not fear her then. We did not think that if it came to war with Russia our struggle would be a struggle to survive. We knew the Marxist dogmas: they did not frighten us. Like Keats, who had the axioms of philosophy in mind, we thought the axioms of history are not true until they are proved upon the pulses, and our pulses did not prove the truth of Marx and Engels. No free man's pulses ever will.

Russia has changed, of course, in these six years. Russia has grown impatient with the timetable of Professor Marx's domesticated Fate and has expedited it where she could by conspiracy and fraud and murder and the intervention of the political police. But Russia has not changed to something other than she was. She is still the nation we knew six years ago. And she is no more our potential master now than she was when the productivity of our people and the skill of our technicians kept her armies in the field and her planes in the air.

What then has changed if it is not Russia? Communism? Is it the capture of the Chinese government by Communists and the pressure of Communist propaganda and armed bands upon the peoples of Southeast Asia which persuades us that we have now no choice but to stand with our backs to the wall?

It is true that the government of China is Communist; that

the most populous country in the world, having thrown off a corrupt, reactionary and brutal regime, has turned, not to self-government and individual freedom, but to government by propaganda and the state police. But tragic as that development is for all who value civilization and freedom, it does not mean that the experience of the six years just past has demonstrated the truth of the Marxist dialectic or proved the inevitability of Communist domination of the earth.

On the contrary, the experience of the past six years has proved the opposite. It has proved in France and throughout Western Europe that if Communism is opposed by the weapons appropriate to the struggle against Communism — by economic and social opportunity rather than by the bombs and bayonets the Republican adolescents would apply to the ills of Asia — Communism cannot score its victories of desperation. If the last six years have demonstrated anything, they have demonstrated that the Marxist Destiny, unlike the Destiny of the Greeks, is not inescapable when men of courage and resource make up their minds to fight it.

Only those who continue obstinately and childishly to regard the crisis in which we live as a military crisis to be won or lost by military weapons can fail to read the vast significance of that victory to which we give the wholly deceptive title of Economic Aid to Europe. When the history of our time is written, if we keep our courage long enough to leave a history, the battle fought in Western Europe with food and credits and materials, under the name of George Marshall and on lines laid down by the present Secretary of State, may well prove to have been one of the decisive battles of mankind.

No, it is not the irrresistible spread of Communism over the earth, or some Phoenix change in Russia, which has altered us in six years' time from a people who believed the future was our future to a people who talk of fighting for survival. And neither is it the shock of the Korean war and the discovery that Asiatic soldiers are men like any others. Only the Old China Hands of the Shanghai bars and the Senate lobbies ever doubted that they were.

The real change as always is neither in our stars nor in our enemies but in ourselves. It is not that Russia is all at once ten times more dangerous but that we see her so. It is not that Marxist dialectic has proved the inevitability of Communist triumph, but that we do not believe, as we once did, in the inevitable triumph of the dialectic of freedom.

If we really wish to understand the difference between the Republic of this day and year and the Republic of the same day six years back, it is that alteration, the alteration in ourselves, we will examine. It is not, I think, a difficult alteration to measure. The difference is not Joe McCarthy or Herbert Hoover or Robert Taft or any of the rest of the timid or calculating men who have succumbed to fear in themselves or exploited fear in others for their partisan or personal advantage. Timidity is not an American characteristic — as those who attempt to live by it politically will learn.

We are not afraid of Russia. We are not afraid of Communism. We are not even afraid of those gastric and imaginary terrors which frighten the Senator from Wisconsin until every face he sees beneath the bed of his political ambition is Communist. McCarthy has done incalculable damage to the tradition of decency and responsibility and mutual respect upon which a free and self-governing society must rest — upon which this society had rested for a hundred and sixty years before his time — but McCarthy is not the author of the decay in American confidence. On the contrary, it is the decay in American confidence which made McCarthy possible. Only a people who found themselves, a few years after their greatest triumph, contemplating the possibility of disaster, and unable to account for the deterioration of their fortunes, would give a moment's thought to reckless and irresponsible accusations made without evidence and offered without proof.

The real reason for the change in the American situation is something considerably more fundamental even than the decay of a political morality. The difference between the United States of 1951 and the United States of 1945 is a difference in the nation itself, in the inward being of the nation, in the sense of purpose and direction which gives vitality and confidence to a life whether it be the life of a nation or the life of a single human being.

Six years ago, and for a decade and more before that, the people of the United States had a common and creative purpose. In the years of the war that purpose, made articulate and comprehensible by Franklin Roosevelt, was a purpose not merely to frustrate the designs of the dictators but to establish a new order of peace and freedom throughout the world — freedom to think, freedom to worship, freedom from want, freedom from fear. Prior to the war, in the decade of the thirties, the national purpose — the purpose at least of a great majority of the people of the country — was a purpose not merely to pull ourselves out of the last and worst of our business depressions, but to create a society in which men could continue to live as men in dignity and freedom without paying the recurrent price of unemployment and the ultimate price of unemployability: a society which would prove that the alternative to economic slavery need not be political slavery, and that a free and responsible human being, thinking and acting for himself, is still a wiser governor of a nation than all the bureaus of the state police.

No one who was alive in this country six years ago or sixteen years ago — no one who was conscious of the Republic in the months before the San Francisco Conference or the months of the emergence of the concept of the New Deal — can doubt, however cynical and sick he may be now, that these purposes were then alive and vigorous in the country, and that the confidence of the country in itself and in its future rested directly upon the universal recognition of the will to act. No one who is conscious of this city and this country today can doubt, either, that these purposes no longer shape our minds, and that our loss of confidence in our future and in ourselves, our desperate talk of struggle for survival, reflect that hollow emptiness at the heart.

Certainly our foreign policy reflects it. We liberals have harsh and often just things to say of that policy. We condemn its defensiveness, its dependence upon the Russian initiative, its reliance upon the concept of containment. Who, we say, can imagine the word "containment" in Roosevelt's mouth? But for all our scorn we know, or ought to know, that the defensiveness of our foreign policy is dictated not by the mentality of the Department of State but by the mentality of the country. The basic orientation of a foreign policy is inevitably determined by the orientation of domestic opinion. If a people thinks defensively about its life at home its foreign policy will necessarily be defensive. If the people of the United States fix their minds upon the preservation of something called their "way of life," meaning the way they imagine they now live, or the way they like to think they lived before, their foreign policy will be directed to the preservation of the status quo elsewhere in the world or even to the restoration of some earlier and vanished status. By the same sign and for the same reason, if the people of the United States should again fix their minds upon the realization of a new and richer life for themselves and for the world, their foreign policy would inevitably become positive and vigorous as the policies of creative and purposeful countries always are.

The truth is that the place to remedy an unsatisfactory foreign policy is not in Formosa or Western Germany but at home. Until the country recovers a sense of national purpose within itself, until it shapes again its national will, its foreign policy must continue to be defensive and Russia must be left the initiative she has held since the war's end. Those who contend the opposite — those who argue that any consideration of American ends, American aims, must wait upon the realization of our aims abroad, and, above all, upon the arming of this country for defense — delude themselves. Their assumption is unsound and the argument they derive from it is inconclusive.

The assumption supposes that the continuing crisis which afflicts our world is primarily a military crisis, and the argument insists that in time of military crisis the unity of parties and opinions is the first objective of policy which must be secured at any cost. A national program within the United States aimed at the realization of American ends — freedom, economic as well as political: equality of opportunity and equality under the law — would, it is argued, divide the country, alienate powerful groups and leave us helpless before our enemies.

The assumption, however, supposes what is not true. The struggle in which we are engaged is not primarily a military struggle. It is primarily a political struggle, a social struggle, which the Russians are waging on their side by conducting a social and political offensive against our institutions and ourselves in every quarter of the world. To trust solely to military means to defend ourselves against such an attack is to lose the war before the battles can be fought — and, it may well be, to expedite the very disaster we seek to prevent. Until we can mount a social and political offensive of our own we cannot successfully defend ourselves, let alone prevail. But an American social and political offensive cannot be mounted to influence the rest of mankind until the American people have committed themselves to its realization in their own country. Merely to be against Communism is not an offensive. It is not even a policy. It is a confession of defeat.

As for the argument deriving from that assumption — the argument that unity is the first requirement in such a time as this, and that no price is too high to pay for it — the answer is simple. The answer is that there is a price too high to pay for unity, and a unity too dubious to purchase at any price. The price too high to pay is the price we are now paying in the United States — the price of spiritual impotence. The unity too dubious to purchase is the unity we have acquired in return — the unity of the reactionaries of both parties in a common intention to paralyze the great creative American tradition of liberalism, leaving the Republic without purpose or direction — leaving the Republic indeed without anything but the bare-bone determination to survive which these blind men tell us we must accept in place of all our hopes, our pride, our confidence, our courage.

No, it is time and past time to face the realities of our situation in the Republic. Everything — our determination abroad, our courage and stamina in the face of the terrible trial which lies before us, our eventual victory in that trial — everything depends upon our undertaking again the achievement of the American dream of a truly free, a truly democratic society: a society in which men shall be equal in opportunity, and equal before the law, not in word only but in fact: a society in which all men may share the security which is now the privilege of some men only: a society in which the inexhaustible human resources of a great and intelligent people may be released for the creative labor which is the dignity of human life. Until we undertake that task we shall not regain the sense of national purpose which is our present and fatal lack. Until we have accomplished some part at least of what we propose we cannot recapture from the Communists the political and social initiative which we must have to win the struggle for the future.

1951

10

The Power of Choice

*In the past it has been our American conviction —
a conviction implicit in our actions rather than explicit
in our words — that history is made by men, not men by
history.*

10

THE POWER OF CHOICE

WHAT IS IN QUESTION in this country is the survival of the American confidence that men can choose the future.

For some time now we have been listening to a national argument which the American press agrees to call the Great Debate. The consensus of opinion seems to be that the press is wrong: that the Great Debate is neither great nor much of a discussion. Senator Wiley's early demand that the highest and most responsible military officer of the Republic be required to testify to what the Senator called personal feelings and private animosities raised understandable doubts as to the elevation of the proceedings. And the effect of the whole dispute on the Congress and the country has been something less than illuminating. When the principal arguments were all in, the popular verdict apparently came to this: that General MacArthur was wholly right and that General MacArthur's opinions were altogether wrong.

Nevertheless the press, for once, was wiser than the people. The confused and interminable altercation now going forward in Washington and in the Republic is, without any doubt whatever, a debate, and the debate deserves the adjective. Upon its issue will depend the kind of country this country is to be.

What is in debate is not merely our policy in the Far East — whether or not the Korean War should have been extended to China. What is in debate is the underlying question General MacArthur was obliged to face when his proposal was challenged on the ground that the extension of the Korean War might mean war with Russia and so a third world war. What is in debate is the view of human history, of the freedom of human choice, which we as Americans are prepared to hold.

In the past it has been our American conviction — a conviction implicit in our actions rather than explicit in our words — that history is made *by men,* not men by history. It is not only possible, we have thought, but a self-evident truth that a free people, if it possesses the virility and the inventiveness and the daring, can choose for itself the kind of world it wishes to live in and then create that world. A free people is capable, that is to say, of the pursuit of happiness — the pursuit of human happiness. We have not believed that men's lives, or the forms of their societies, or the future to which they are committed are determined in advance by the patterns of the stars or the prophecies of the books or the necessities of the blood or the character of the countryside into which men are born, or even by the laws of economics. Above all, we have not believed, as older societies believed before us, that the events of human history — either disasters *or* triumphs — are inevitable.

The whole idea of the inevitable has been repugnant to us. Nothing, we have opined, is inevitable but death and taxes. Anything else in the world can be changed, including — including particularly — the prophecies. Anything else can be changed and, for the most part, has been: forms of government, dogmas of belief, methods of husbandry, habits of life — even the man himself: even the compulsion of the blood, the shape of the head, the length and weight of the body, and the color of the hair. We have had no respect for fate: we worshiped God, not fate. We have had no particular reverence for history: we believed in men, not history. History was the history men made, not the veiled divinity that told them what they had to be.

Our confidence, in brief, was in the future. Which is to say that our confidence was in the power of human choice to make the future. We considered that a free people can make the future for itself: master its destiny.

That was the American position: the position made evident in our actions from the first movement west across the continent; made articulate sometimes also in our words. We had no illusions about the orthodoxy of our view. We knew perfectly well that the great majority of mankind disagreed with us and always had. The orthodox conception of man's place in the universe, man's relation to time and to event, had always been the very different conception that man is the victim of the inevitable, whose only escape from the ineluctable design is to accept it. The authors of that reckless and willful phrase about the pursuit of happiness in the Declaration of American Independence had every reason to know how their affirmation would be received in older, wiser, and less courageous countries. We have learned since, throughout the history of our literature, how stubborn, how bitter, and how vindictive that reaction can be: how scornfully the believers in fate can speak of our precarious belief in man and in man's future; how sneeringly the servants of determinism can dispose of our "idea of progress," as they choose to call it; how contemptuously the worshipers of certainty can dismiss our self-confidence, our self-reliance, above all the rash impiety of our willingness to think for ourselves, and say as we think, and do as we say.

Nevertheless, and until this time, we have held to our convictions. We have nourished an inarticulate belief that there is a relation of some kind between the individual human freedom we mean to have and the rejection of the dogma of inevitability. Freedom and inevitability, we have thought, cannot live together. No nation can be free which does not keep the future open in its people's minds.

Now, it appears, we are no longer certain. The world has changed. The dogma of inevitability has made new converts throughout half the earth, and the menace of their fanatic faith has made still further converts, even among us. Fear has accomplished what persuasion never could. Americans — many Americans it seems — are ready to accept the doctrine of inevitability for themselves and to force it on their fellow citizens. Unless we accept the inevitable, they tell us, the inevitable will destroy *us*. And the country listens, ponders, doubts. And the issue is joined. The petty debate over the personality of a man becomes the great debate over the destiny of the Republic.

The MacArthur controversy is, of course, the occasion of the Great Debate, not the cause. General MacArthur did not invent the view of human history he apparently accepts. The controversy which centers on his name has, however, posed the underlying issue in terms which no one can mistake, and has related it to a decision which the country, largely because of the controversy, can no longer avoid. That decision is a decision affecting our survival as a people and, very probably, the survival of our world.

Only on the surface is the difference between MacArthur and his critics a military difference. Actually it is a difference of belief, a difference of essential philosophy: a difference touching the freedom of the people of the United States to *choose*, in the greatest dilemma they have ever faced. Fundamentally what General MacArthur and General Bradley disagree about is the freedom of the people of the United States to pursue their traditional policy of peace *and* the defense of human liberty in the modern world. To General MacArthur the risk of Russian intervention and, so, of world war should not deter us from extending the Korean War to China and winning a "victory," because the risk of Russian intervention has already been taken: because events, that is to say, are out of our hands. To General Bradley, the chance of Russian intervention *should* deter us because events are *not* out of our hands: because, as the General puts it, we have avoided war with Russia thus far and if we can continue to avoid it long enough we may be able to avoid it altogether.

Neither general knows or pretends to know what Russia will actually do. Both agree that Russia may attack us at any moment — that the rulers of Russia will be restrained neither by humanity nor by moral scruple: only by fear. Both are aware that the Russians themselves regard war between the Soviets and the United States as inevitable: their doctrine of economic determinism makes it so. The difference between the two men is a difference as to our freedom of action under these circumstances. To one, we can still choose between the struggle for freedom and peace on the one hand and world war on the other; to the second, we are already, in effect, at war: the millstones are turning, the grain must be ground.

This is the difference also between the two opinions which have been formed, regardless of party, behind the principal figures of the debate. Those on the one side talk in terms of what they call "realism" and "courage," by which they mean the "realistic" acceptance of the inevitability of war, and the "courageous" adoption in China and, presumably, elsewhere of a policy based upon the unblinking recognition of that fact. Those on the other continue to talk in terms of hope, contending that we have not yet lost control of the great election between peace and war: that it is still possible, if we have the courage and the patience, to avoid world war on the one hand and Communist domination of the earth on the other.

To men of the second opinion there is room for maneuver in the narrow strait between these two dangers. We can make ourselves too strong to attack and too important to the world to isolate: the party of peace and the fortress of power; the standard of effective freedom to which men, still free, can rally. We can gain allies for ourselves and arm them. We can strengthen the economy of the free world and build backfires of hope in the exploited areas where hunger and despair make tinder for the Russian torch. We can put together regional alliances — strong points of mutual confidence such as the Atlantic Pact — within the structure of the United Nations and find means to give the defeated peoples of Germany and Japan a stake in the common future. We can implement the Charter of the United Nations by building out of the United Nations command which already exists in Korea a permanent United Nations police force and so enlist the universal longing for peace behind our purposes rather than the purposes of the Russians. We can turn our faces toward a free and peaceful future for the world, planning it, organizing it as we can under the Point Four program or otherwise, giving mankind a measure of hope instead of a certainty of slaughter, and so breaking the evil spell the Russians, with their alternatives of spiritual slavery, or inevitable war, have woven.

To men who hold the first opinion — to the "realists" — all this is folly if not actually something worse than folly. It is folly to talk of avoiding war: we are already at war. So MacArthur: so Wedemeyer. It is nonsense to concern ourselves about what our allies think: our allies have no choice, they will think as we think or go without. So MacArthur: so

the McCormick-McCarthy fringe. It is ridiculous to offer
relief to suffering peoples: there is no time for relief — we
cannot even be sure the grain we send to the starving in India
will help *us*. As for the United Nations and regional alliances
and the Atlantic Pact — all this is legalistic trifling. In the
last analysis there are only the Russians and ourselves. The
chips are down. The time has come to act: to act in China —
to act wherever action is necessary — to act, that is, by force.

It is this later position which reveals the true issue of the
Great Debate. If you ask the "realists" *why* the chips are
down; *why* there is no time; *why* war with Russia and hence
world war is inevitable, they will reply, many of them: Because
the *Russians* are committed; because the *Russians* will allow
us no time; because the *Russians* say war is inevitable. But
this can hardly be the actual reason. No American believes,
and least of all the patriotic Americans who urge this view
upon the country, that the Russians possess the exclusive
power to decide the future for us all: that American intentions
no longer count in the great decision. Certainly no American
who knows the facts of record could believe anything so
humiliating to his country and so false. It has yet to be demonstrated that American determination and persistence,
backed by American strength and the strength of our friends
in the free world, are incapable of deterring the Russians
from an action which would precipitate the most terrible of
all wars — a war fought with the weapons of extermination.
On the contrary, the facts of record powerfully suggest that
the Russians have already been deterred and may be deterred
again.

No, the real reason why the advocates of this opinion believe in the inevitability of a war which has thus far been
avoided — a war which no one wants and every decent man
must dread for the world's sake if not for his own — the real

reason why the advocates of this opinion believe in the inevitablity of war is that they accept the inevitability of war *as dogma*. War between the United States and Soviet Russia is inevitable to them, not because we cannot continue to avoid it in the future as we have in the past, regardless of Russian desires, but because war between the United States and Soviet Russia is *inevitable*. It is not that they "want" war. MacArthur's partisans are no more the war party than Truman and Acheson and Marshall and Bradley are friends of the Communists. Both characterizations are insults to the public intelligence. MacArthur is doubtless as honest in saying that he hates war as Acheson in demonstrating by the record of his office that he has been one of the foremost opponents of Communism. But MacArthur and his supporters, however they may hate war, accept it. They accept it as "already here." They accept it as inescapable. They accept it as inevitable *in the nature of things*. They accept it for reasons beyond reason. And, accepting it, they reject as weakness, or as folly, or as what they call appeasement, the notion that the United States can continue to avoid war and still stand firm: that a free people can shape the future for itself even in a world which holds the Russians: that men can master their destiny even though destiny presents itself in the vast, impersonal terms in which it shows itself to us, and even though whole peoples make a religion of submission to it.

Whether General MacArthur's "realists" realize it or not, it is their position and not the position of their opponents which approximates the philosophy they detest — the philosophy all decent men detest. The dogma of the inevitability of war between the United States and Russia is Communist dogma. Its origins are Marxist. Long before it was orthodox belief among MacArthur's followers here, it was orthodox belief among the Communists in Russia. A full generation ago when the economic and political interests of the United States and the Soviet Union conflicted nowhere on earth and no American newspaper publisher — not even the most unprincipled — shouted for a Russian War, war between Russia and the United States was already official doctrine in the Soviet Union. The Commissars had consulted the oracles. The sacred viscera had been observed. The holy texts had been deciphered and the flight of birds. War was in the tarot cards and war would therefore come. Why? Because the theory said so. Because the words were written in the book.

The whole proposition was, in its origin, a product of authoritarian superstition — a superstition which reads the future of mankind in the tea leaves of the economic systems: war or peace, life or death. And it was by authoritarian propagation that it was domesticated in this country. The first to tell us that war between the Soviet Union and the United States was inevitable were former Communists: men who had left the discipline of the Communist Party but had not lost the habit of the Party's thought. And the first to welcome the assurance were those in the United States whose inclination had always been authoritarian and who found authoritarian ideas — even the ideas of their enemies — more palatable than a traditional American liberalism they had never understood.

Indeed, even at the present moment, the propagation of the dogma of inevitable war by certain politicans and certain publishers pursues the authoritarian pattern. Those who criticize the dogma are to be silenced. An Administration policy aimed at the avoidance of war is to be discredited as motivated by Communist sympathy if not actually by subversive purpose. Advocacy of peace is to be stigmatized as treason to the United States. All the full Communist doctrine of the inevitability of war between the United States and Russia is to be forced upon the country as American doctrine until —

ultimate irony — all who refuse to accept it can be denounced as Communists.

What the consequence of the Great Debate will be in terms of military policy is not, I think, in doubt. The country plainly prefers our present attempt to shape a future narrowly for ourselves between the two disasters of war and Communism to any "realistic" alternative thus far advanced. Indeed the country would welcome a determined and an idealistic effort to make that future more truly ours in place of the mere negation of Communism which we seem now to intend. We do not want war with Russia or with anyone else, and we will avoid war so long as it is in our power to do so. We are not yet convinced that we have lost that power.

But whether, in rejecting the proposal now before us, we will reject also the authoritarian philosophy on which that proposal rests, depends upon our willingness to see what the issue of the Great Debate actually is.

Those who would impose the dogma of inevitable war as the determining consideration in the great decision we have to make are so vociferous in their claims of superior patriotism that they may confuse the actual issue in the minds of many men. The actual issue is whether we still believe, in a time of totalitarian governments and authoritarian ideologies and the mechanization of human life, in the proposition which the founders of this Republic regarded as self-evident: whether we still believe that history is lived by men, not men by history; whether we still regard the future as open to our aspirations, not foreclosed to us by our fate; whether we still think of the "arable field of events" — Keats's great phrase — as arable by men, not frozen around them by an icy will; whether we still consider mankind to be capable of the pursuit of happiness or whether we have grown ashamed of that highhearted language and think of men now as mechanical figures helpless in the predetermined web of time.

The actual issue, that is to say, is the issue which torments our generation everywhere: the choice between the belief in ourselves and the belief in authority, in the predetermination of events. It was never, perhaps, in human history, more difficult or more dangerous for men to believe in themselves. But it was also never more necessary — never more necessary, surely, for us in the United States. For unless we can hope, unless we can keep the future open, unless we can continue to believe in our power to shape the future for ourselves, the future will be war and the war will be destruction for the world. It is, to me at least, inconceivable that in a country in which the tradition of belief in man is as vigorous as it is with us — a country shaped, indeed, by that tradition — the dogma of inevitability should take hold. And yet the seed is here. The labor is to crush it.

1951

11

The Belief in Man

It is necessary to believe in man, not only as the Christians believe in man, out of pity, or as the democrats believe in man, out of loyalty, but also as the Greeks believed in man, out of pride.

11

THE BELIEF IN MAN

OUR TIME HAS ASKED US two great questions — a question
of government for the governors and a question of education
for the teachers.

How do you govern in the new world with its invisible
frontiers? And how do you educate the new people with their
new possibilities of creation and destruction?

We used to say twenty-five years ago that the world couldn't
survive another war. We thought we were making speeches.
We know now that we were stating fact. The only parts of
the world which will survive this war, except as ruins and
fragments and remains, will be the parts of the world over
which the war has not been fought. Next time, as the Nazis
have obligingly shown us, there will be no margins. Planes
which flew a few hundred miles with a few pounds of explosives in 1918 now fly thousands of miles with tons of explosives. Robot projectiles which now carry a ton of explosives
a couple of hundred miles will increase both range and load
in much the same way.

The lesson we have learned over the last few years is the
lesson that "there are no neutrals in this war." In the next war
— if there is a next war — the lesson we shall learn will be
the lesson that there is no part of the world which is not a
battlefield. Which means, not as a figure of speech but as a
statement of fact, that what we understand by "the world"

will not survive that war. Which means, in turn, that if there is another war our world is lost. Which means, finally, that we have no future worth thinking about unless we can learn, and learn quickly, to govern the world in such a way, and to educate its people in such a way, that another war will not occur.

When anyone talks about the crisis of humanism at the war's end, he is talking, if he is serious, about the answer humanism has to give, or ought to have to give, or ought to be allowed to have to give, to these two inescapable and desperate questions of government and education. He is not talking, that is to say, about the sad plight of the classics in the modern college, or the overemphasis on science in the current curriculum, or the lamentable discovery, in universities which had previously terminated all literature with the last rock on Land's End, that an American literature also exists. He is not talking, that is to say, in terms of academic politics or academic prestige or his own future as a professor. Above all, he is not talking about the effect of the Army training program on the academic economic system.

He is talking about the most urgent and most critical decisions to be taken in his time. And he is saying that a certain approach to these problems, a certain tradition of thought, a certain discipline, has something of importance to offer to their solution. He is saying that the tendency of the practical men among his contemporaries to exclude that approach and that discipline is dangerous. He is saying that it is dangerous, not to him and his academic fellows only, but to the practical men themselves — and to the world they share with us.

The serious question in all this discussion of the humanities, in other words, is the question whether the humanists and their discipline have, in fact, anything to offer to the solution of the two great moral and intellectual and political problems we must solve or perish. If they have not, if the humanists can claim no more than a decorative function in the preparation of young men for dinners-in-hall, then their disputes with their academic rivals, however brilliantly managed and however learnedly expressed, are hardly worth the present attention of living men. For one thing, living men have other and more urgent business to attend to. For another, they have every reason to remark that a philosophy of the education and life of man which has nothing to say to mankind about its life and education at the most critical moment in its recorded history is not a philosophy of man at all but a dilettantism with a pretentious name.

Both problems clearly fall within the field of humanist concern. Certainly the question of the role of education in the crisis of our time is a question on which the humanists can be expected to speak and by which they should expect to be judged. Humanism is at bottom a theory of the education proper to man and cannot therefore avoid judgment upon its position in the most solemn examination of educational theory the modern world has been obliged to undertake. On the contrary, humanism might well protest, and bitterly protest, its exclusion from that great assize.

The same thing is true, or so it seems to me, of the problem of government. Humanists, I realize, have not claimed the right in recent years to speak with authority of the art of government. Some of them may even decline that right today. Some of them, thinking of humanism as though it were something in a university catalogue, may perhaps refuse to hold opinions on the art of government — on the ground that government is taught in the courses on political science and that the courses on political science are not usually given in the departments of humanities.

Others, taking a less curricular view, might conceivably renounce all right to be heard on the issue of government, and might decline to be judged by their contribution to its solution, on the ground that humanism is concerned with men solely as individuals and not with men in their relation to each other, or on the ground that humanism looks inward, not outward, or on the ground that humanism looks backward, not forward.

Philosophers of the ancient world would consider these to be strange limitations, I submit, upon the spiritual jurisdiction of a school which concerns itself with *humanitas* — with those things in man which are most manlike. Aulus Gellius defined *humanitas* by saying that earnest students of the liberal arts are most highly humanized because the knowledge they pursue is "granted to man alone of all the animals." Of the various forms of knowledge granted to man alone of all the animals, knowledge of the art of government is surely not the least.

Nor was it the least regarded in the past. It was not believed in Athens and Rome that the best education for man was an education unrelated to his practice of the art of government. On the contrary, it was assumed that a philosophy which thought in terms of the whole man, of the man in whom the manlike qualities were most developed, must necessarily have views not only on the training of those qualities but upon their exercise as well, and above all upon their noblest exercise — which would have included, in that time and in those cities, their exercise in government.

But there are other reasons than reasons of logic and history for the extension of humanistic jurisdiction, and therefore of humanistic responsibility, to the art of government. There are reasons of a practical nature. The humanistic renunciation of the public world has been happy neither for the public world nor for humanism. Humanism has become pallid with the pallor of all things grown within ivory walls; and government, once considered a noble art, has become at best a kind of profession and at worst a business. The recent uproar about Henry Wallace makes the point with an unintentional but appalling pertinence. Henry Wallace, said a characteristic article by one of the best-known of American journalists, is an exceptionally fine human being. He has a feeling for the tendency of things to come. But he is not at home and at ease in "the real world" and he is therefore, under the circumstances of the election, unacceptable for the Vice-Presidency.

Whatever may be said of the judgment of Henry Wallace, the view of statesmanship there expressed is one a humanist might challenge and, in my opinion, should. Indeed both humanism and statesmanship would be healthier today if the humanists had challenged the businessman's view of the art of government before it produced the generations of leaders "at home in the real world" which conducted Western civilization through so much of the nineteenth century and the twentieth to the situation in which we find ourselves today. It might be difficult to prove that there would have been more Lincolns and Jeffersons if the humanists had not forsaken the public world, but it must be obvious that there would almost certainly have been fewer Coolidges and Tafts.

I propose to assume, therefore, and for the purposes of this discussion, that humanism can be expected to supply an answer to the two critical questions of how to govern and how to teach. It remains therefore to consider whether the answer humanism can be expected to offer is or is not entitled to a better hearing than it has had.

But that consideration turns, of course, upon the nature

of the humanist answer. There are almost as many definitions
of humanism and the humanities as there are men who have
written them. If one assumes, for example, that the humanities are what Webster calls "the branches of polite learning,"
especially belles-lettres and the ancient classics, and that
humanism is merely a scholarly devotion to these studies, there
will be some difficulty in persuading a tortured world that
humanism and the humanities have much to say to it.

Polite learning, it will be objected, is all very well for a
polite age, and knowledge of the ancient classics and of
beautiful letters is a charming embellishment in a serene and
spacious time: but for us, bewildered and frightened in a
chaotic and savage world in which all the landmarks are lost
and all the assurances washed away, the book beneath the
classic bough is a mockery and a delusion. We have First
Things to learn again before we can learn Last Things. We
must learn again how to survive — how to keep the peace:
how to restrain the wild beasts and the violence. Keep your
culture, the world might well say, until we can build a quiet
room to house it in — until we can be certain that the house
of culture will stand at least for a generation at a time: until
the skies are quiet again and a place for stars, not for the
most terrible and insensate death and the swiftest destruction.

And there will be much the same objection if you define
your humanist as the perfect type of intellectual aristocrat,
living a life of reflection and criticism above the battle and
the common dust. You will be told that such a man, if he does
not make himself a prig in the process, may well become
an ornament in a world which has room for ornaments, but
that we, who must buttress and rebuild our lives before chaos
engulfs them, have no time to think of such luxuries as a
natural aristocracy of learning and of taste.

So again if you adopt the definition of humanism which

describes it as a form of intellectual discipline — the discipline of the intellect for its own sake rather than for the sake of proficiency in some art, or craft, or profession. Rude persons will tell you that to cultivate the mind for its own sake one must first have leisure, and that to have leisure one must be able to foretell the time, and that in our world a man cannot foretell the time since the time is already past and nothing is sure and each day is more dangerous than the last and a man can only prepare himself for disaster or survival.

It will be the same, too, even if you take the more generous definition in which humanism appears as that method of education and that practice of life of which the purpose is to free the faculties of men for their fullest exercise and their finest development. To free the faculties of men for their fullest exercise is a noble purpose. But its end, as someone will be unkind enough to point out, is not a free man — a man committed to freedom as well as possessed of it — but rather a *freed* man — a man freed of all commitments, including the commitment to freedom itself.

Such an end, however enchanting it may seem in a peaceful time when men can afford the after-dinner sport of questioning everything and giving themselves to nothing, has an irresponsible and even a frivolous look to a generation which has been compelled to think of freedom as something you were either prepared to die for or prepared to lose. To be free of every prejudice, including the prejudice of freedom, may make a man superior, but it can hardly endear him, for the moment at least, to those who have offered their lives precisely to defend the prejudice that freedom has a supreme and absolute worth. Moral eclecticism looks curiously out of place among the dead wreaths and the fading cotton flags of the soldiers' cemeteries. It is particularly out of place when the certainty of the soldier's grave that freedom was worth dying for is the only certainty men have to hold to. To offer to teach the men of such a generation how to avoid the pitfalls of prejudice and excessive belief is indeed to offer stones to those who starve for bread.

The fact is that the humanism of these various definitions is a humanism which finds its reason in the fifteenth century rather than our own — in the fifteenth century and in those later centuries in which, as in the fifteenth, the sickness of the soul was dogma and superstition. Humanism considered as an intellectual discipline-for-discipline's-sake, or as a regimen to free the mind of prejudice and infatuation, or as an aristocratic training of the taste, or as a cult of the classic past, or as the appreciation of fine arts and beautiful letters, is a prime specific for such ills as bigotry and puritanism and jesuitry and vulgarity and Victorianism and the complacency of the bourgeois mind. But humanism so conceived has little if anything to say to a time in which the spiritual sickness is not excess of belief but lack of belief. And ours, if we understand the ills we suffer from, is such a time.

We have valued liberty enough to fight for it, and we know very well what enemy we detest, but the affirmative cause, not only of the war but of our lives, escapes us. When we debate, as we have debated endlessly, the question of what we are fighting for, we have sometimes thought it was what we are living for we needed most to know. We have seen whole peoples deliver their lives and purposes and wills to tyrants they themselves have invented out of a loud voice and a blathering mouth and a ridiculous uniform to satisfy the hunger of their fear. We have seen others who cried out for a great conversion of the world, a vast revival, a wind from beyond the planet and the stars, to fill us in spite of ourselves, and without our effort, by some miracle of faith, like the miracle they imagine to have happened when Christianity first took the world, or when the religion of the Prophet took it.

Everywhere in our time there are the signs and indications of a passion to believe, a passion to escape from the sense of human inadequacy which spreads and deepens as science and the mechanical arts disclose the enormous scale and the terrible potentialities of a universe vaster and more dangerous than men, before our generation, had imagined. The natural sciences open fissures in the skin of the earth and the cover of the sky which lead beyond human meaning. The specialists press their narrow drills of research outward and away from the human center of experience. The libraries overflow with a flood of printed pages, and knowledge has become too vast for men to know.

The world, we say to ourselves, is too large for us, too difficult to understand, too savage to restrain, too swift to master. It is no longer a world to be measured in distance by a man's foot, or in time by a man's sleeping and waking, or in danger by a man's strength or an animal's. It is a world beyond the capacity of men to control — a world that needs gods or men like gods. And so we long for the men like gods, or for the gods, to believe in.

Humanists may regret this hunger to believe, but they will be foolish, notwithstanding, if they ignore the longing of their generation; and worse than foolish if they do not see the significance of that longing to themselves and to their cause. For the meaning of our longing for belief is this: that we have lost our sense of the place of man in the universe.

It is to a generation which has lost this sense that the humanists now must offer what they have to teach. If they do not understand the significance of that fact to the philosophy they protest; if they persist in declaring that what they have to teach is a method only, a gymnastic, or at the best an antidote, a cleansing salt, an antiseptic; if they are unwilling to turn their questions into answers for a time that needs their answers — then they have themselves to thank, and not the blunders of the Army and the Navy, or the blindness of their colleagues in the universities, for the indifference of which they now complain.

For there is a definition of humanism by which humanism becomes a belief in the one thing in which man has greatest need now to believe — himself, and the dignity and importance of the place he fills in the world he lives in. There is a definition of humanism by which humanism becomes precisely the belief of man in his own dignity, in his essential worth as a man, in what Ralph Barton Perry calls "his characteristic perfection"; a belief not in the potentiality of man, but in the actuality of man; a belief not in the classic perfection of the beautiful letters men have written in the distant past, but in the human perfection of the men who wrote those letters and of others like them, whether writers or others than writers, and whether living in the past or in the present or not yet born; a belief not in the thing a man may become if he reads the right books and develops the right tastes and undergoes the right discipline, but a belief in the thing he is.

No one has put this better than Professor Perry in his superb *Definition of the Humanities*. "The reference to man in the context of the so-called 'humanities,'" he says, "is . . . not descriptive or apologetic, but eulogistic; not 'human — all too human,' or 'only human,' but human in the sense in which one deems it highest praise to be called 'a man.'" The answer humanism has it in its power to make to the two great questions, how to govern and how to teach, is the answer of belief in man, "in the sense in which one deems it highest praise to be called 'a man.' " If the world can be taught to believe in the worth of man, in the dignity of man, in the "characteristic perfection" of man, it can be taught not only to survive but to live. If the world can be governed in belief in the worth of man, in the dignity of man, it can be governed in peace.

These propositions need no proof. They speak for themselves. If government throughout the world were directed by a convinced belief in the dignity of man as man, in the worth of man as man, so that decisions of government were everywhere made in consonance with that belief and in furtherance of it, no one can doubt that the world would be well governed and that peace would be as nearly certain as peace can be in a variable universe. It is lack of faith in the essential dignity and worth of man which corrupts and weakens democratic governments, substituting for a government by the people in the people's interest, which is peace, a government of rulers in the rulers' interest — which may be war. It is doubt of the dignity and worth of man which opens the road to the tyrannies and dictatorships which have no choice but war. It is cynical contempt for the worth and dignity of man which makes the wars of the dictators wars of slavery and subjugation.

If the fundamental proposition upon which the government of the world was based were the proposition that man, because he is man, and in his essential quality as man, has worth and value which governments exist to serve and to protect, regardless of race and regardless of color or religion, there would be litle room for the play of international politics which, under color of realism or under color of necessity, puts power first or oil first or gold first, and men second or nowhere, preparing thus for the wars of power or of oil or gold. If the first business of government everywhere were man, the whole

man of the humanists; if the first object of government everywhere were the good of man, man "in the sense in which one
deems it highest praise to be called 'a man' "; if the first
principle of government everywhere were the principle that
government exists for man and not man for government, there
would be no place for the governments of which the first
business is business, or for the governments of which the first
object is economic advantage, or for the governments of which
the first principle is power.

But to govern in this way it is necessary first of all to
believe, and not merely to declare that one believes, in the
fundamental worth and value of man and to practice that
belief and never to cease to practice it. It is necessary to
believe in man, not only as the Christians believe in man, out
of pity, or as the democrats believe in man, out of loyalty,
but also as the Greeks believed in man, out of pride.

The same thing is true of the question how to teach. If
education were informed with a belief in the dignity and
worth of man; if the purpose of education were an understanding not only of the weaknesses of man and the sicknesses
of man and the failures of man but of the essential nobility of
man also, of his "characteristic perfection," men would be
able again to occupy their lives and to live in the world as
the Greeks lived in it, free of the bewilderment and frustration
which has sent this generation, like the Gadarene swine, squeal-
ing and stumbling and drunk with the longing for immolation,
to hurl themselves into the abysses of the sea.

If science were taught, not as something external to man,
something belittling of man, but as one of the greatest of the
creations of the human spirit: if economics were taught not as
a structure of deterministic laws superior to man and controlling his conduct, but as one of the many mirrors man has

constructed to observe the things he does: if history and descriptive literature were taught not as peep-holes through which the unworthy truth about mankind may be observed but as expressions of man's unique ability and willingness to see and judge himself; if belief in man and in his dignity and worth became the controlling principle of education, so that the people of the world were taught to respect the common principle of humanity in others and in themselves, and to believe that their lives would be shaped and their future determined not by some law of economics, or by some formula of science, or by some regimen of the subconscious, but by their own wills and on their own responsibility — if these things could be accomplished, who will doubt that the sense of irresponsibility and frustration which has driven so many millions of our contemporaries down the blind steep of slavery into war could be corrected?

The task education must accomplish, if free societies are to continue to exist, is the re-creation of the sense of individual responsibility — which means the re-establishment of the belief of men in man. Fascism is only another name for the sickness and desperation which overcome a society when it loses its sense of responsibility for its own life and surrenders its will to a tyrant it, and it alone, has invented. But the sense of responsibility in a nation is a sense of responsibility in the individuals who compose that nation, for the sense of responsibility is always a charge upon the individual conscience and vanishes when many share it. And to re-create the sense of individual responsibility it is necessary to restore the belief of men in man — the belief that man can direct his destiny if he will.

It is impossible to charge the consciences of men with responsibility for the world they live in without convincing them that they can act upon their world — that the power to decide and act is theirs. No one knew that better than Abraham Lincoln, who knew many things about the human soul. When it became necessary for him, in the terrible December of 1862, to drive home to the Congress a sense of its responsibility, he used these words: "Fellow citizens, we cannot escape history. We of this Congress and this Administration will be remembered in spite of ourselves. No personal significance or insignificance can spare one or another of us. The fiery trial through which we pass will light us down, in honor or dishonor, to the latest generation. . . . We — even we here — hold the power and bear the responsibility."

What education in the free countries must drive home, if the free countries are to survive, is the conviction that we — even we here — hold the power and bear the responsibility. The task is in part a task beyond the power of the schools as such, for the sense of individual responsibility and power involves a sense of individual participation, and a sense of individual participation is only possible in a society in which individuals can make themselves felt directly and not through agglomerations of money or people. There must be social changes as well as educational changes. But the educational changes come first. Not until men believe that the responsibility can be theirs to bear, and therefore should be theirs to bear, will they make it theirs. To teach men to believe in themselves therefore is to teach them responsibility and so to assure their freedom.

These, as I understand humanism, are the answers the humanists have it in their power to give to their time and to the questions their time has asked of them. They are answers which seem to me to be true and to dispose, once and for all, of the question whether humanism has anything to say to the generation to which we belong. Any school, any philosophy, which can go as close to the root of the essential sickness of our time has a right to be heard, and may claim that right, and may denounce fairly and justly those who deprive it of that right, pretending that other points of view are more practical and therefore more important.

But these answers are not the answers, as I read the record, which the humanists — all the humanists at least — are willing to give. On the contrary, many humanists would reject them, and reject them for a reason which goes very deep. They would reject them because the dignity of man in which they believe is not the dignity implicit in these answers — is not, that is to say, a dignity which men possess because they are men, but only a dignity which men may earn by undergoing certain disciplines and acquiring certain characteristics.

Man, to these humanists, is not born with worth, but may acquire worth. Until he has earned it he has no right or reason to believe in himself, nor should a belief in man determine the attitude in which he is to be ruled. Humanism to these humanists, in other words, is not a democratic doctrine on which a practice of self-government can be founded, but an aristocratic doctrine which, because its concern is inward, has little to say of government of any kind. It is, if anything, a doctrine opposed to democracy and to theories of the universal worth of man, because excellence, not equality, is its goal and purpose.

It would be a mistake to dismiss these humanists as dwellers in towers, or their definitions as definitions of refuge. The passion for excellence can be a sword as well as a sanctuary. Committed to the love of the arts and the great books and the monuments of unaging intellect, as Yeats so wonderfully called them, and the courtesies and graces and perceptions of a civilized and generous life, the worshipers of excellence have waged war, and noble war, against an increasing vulgarity which has won its greatest triumphs in our time, having found the mechanical means at last to intrude its coarseness into every hour, however private, and every chamber, however secret, of our lives.

Those to whom humanism is the worship of excellence do not admit, as they look around them in the streets and trains and hotel lobbies of our world, that all men have dignity and worth. They do not believe, as they look back across the centuries to the world they imagine to have existed in Athens and in Rome, that all men are able to govern themselves or should be allowed to. They do not agree, as they face the crisis of our time, that freedom is the answer to everything. They do not necessarily hold with public freedom. The freedom they seek is inward in the large and lofty world of enlightened intellect where learning paints the various landscape and a trained and delicate taste selects the road. That there must be peace and quiet outside the mind, if a man is to journey within it, they readily admit. But the peace without, they say, is not their business.

It is understandable enough that men should love what these men love, and hate what they hate. Their ideal of the truly civilized man is in every way admirable. Their contempt for a world in which taste is determined in advertising agencies, and intelligence is measured by the answers children give to questions on the air, is a contempt which later generations of Americans will not find strange. But what is not understandable is their choice of the word humanism to describe their inward and selective life. Humanism as a word cannot cut itself off from its root or forget its derivation. Humanism, to deserve the *humanitas* from which it comes, must incorporate some notion of things appropriate to every man as man — things worthy of man in every man.

It must incorporate, that is to say, some notion of a universal dignity which men possess as men and by virtue of their manhood. The dignity of man upon which a philosophy of man, a school devoted to man, is based cannot be a rare and sought-for attribute which only the school can teach man to acquire and only the philosophy aid man to deserve. You do not construct out of the airy goal at which you hope to arrive the solid ground from which you depart. You do not derive the dignity of man on which your philosophy is founded from the dignity which those few who practice your philosophy can claim to possess. The dignity of man is either here and now or it is never. It is either in mankind or it is nowhere.

One can no more make an aristocracy of human dignity than one can make an aristocracy of human love or human curiosity, or any other fundamental human characteristic. Some men will develop their manlike qualities farther than others. Some will be more learned, have surer taste, livelier imagination, greater gentility — will be, in brief, more civilized than others. But whatever the degree of their development, the qualities with which the true humanist is concerned are the manlike qualities — the qualities which men possess because they are men; the qualities, therefore, which all men possess to one degree or another. It is man whom the humanist values, and man is in all men — *is* all men.

To limit humanism, therefore — to put a narrower construction upon it than this — is quite literally to deprive it of its fundamental meaning. It is as though a select association of superior and cultivated people were to call themselves the association of mankind. The word mankind, in such a context, would have an ironic meaning or have none at all. So humanism, if its concern is not man, and therefore all men, has only an ironic meaning or has none. But founded on the universal human basis which its root implies, the name becomes a noble and intelligible word with meanings which our time needs more than any others.

This war is a war against those who, in contempt of man and in despair of man's power to direct his life, have surrendered their lives into the hands of tyrants they themselves have created. It is a war against the philosophy of contempt for man and despair of his future which those who have surrendered their lives have invented to justify themselves, or have accepted from their masters. It is a war therefore in which the issue is, in last analysis, the issue of man — of the concept of man which is to shape and control our time; of the idea of man which governments are to reflect and societies to mirror.

We, on our side, have found it easy to put our cause into negative words, into words of resistance. We are opposed to the philosophy of contempt for man and to those who accept that philosophy: we have seen what it does to those who practice it and to those upon whom it is practiced also. But we have not found it easy to put our cause into the affirmative words of our own purpose. And for this reason: that the affirmative statement of our cause is a declaration of belief in man, and we have not been altogether ready and willing to make that declaration, since we too have felt the winds of fear and doubt which turned our enemies to disbelievers. More than anything else, we need a rebirth of belief in ourselves as men. If humanism will make itself the instrument of that renaissance of man, its place, not only in the universities but in the world, is sure. For if it will make itself that instrument it will give our time its cause.

1944

12

The Act of Faith

For the great central fact before us, the fact to which the evangelists of war have shut their eyes, is . . . the fact that a new and wholly different world is in the process of creating in our time.

12

THE ACT OF FAITH

To EDUCATE AT ALL is to profess a faith in the future of the most explicit kind, since education, by its nature, assumes the future. To make a new beginning in education — and in educational institutions a new administration is always a new beginning, for it is by this method that educational institutions, like other shell-forming organisms, achieve their growth — to make a new beginning in education is to reaffirm that profession of faith, and to reassert it in a new confidence for the years ahead. Neither a new president, nor her officers, nor her trustees, nor her students could commit themselves to a new administration of the college unless they believe in the future — unless they believed that there would be a future — unless they believed that there was still *time*.

And yet, if we may trust what we hear, and what we ourselves say, and what goes on echoing in our minds even in this room and even at this moment, the people of this country have no such confidence. If we may trust what we hear, and what we find ourselves saying, and what our newspapers and our politicians tell us morning after morning, evening after evening, it is our conviction, both as a people and as a government, that we are already engaged in an ineluctable struggle for survival, with force or the threat of force as the necessary

NOTE: Adapted from an address at the inauguration of Margaret Clapp as president of Wellesley College.

weapons — and those weapons so implacably destructive that they may well wipe out all human life across an entire continent, not inconceivably our own.

So convinced are we of the impossibility of a peaceful settlement that talk about the negotiation of peace is discouraged as wishful thinking by the Democratic Department of State on one side, and denounced as subversive activity by certain Republican politicians and newspapers on the other.

So sure are we of the inevitability of conflict that a small group of Senators and members of Congress, undistinguished and unrespected men but raucously self-assured of their political sagacity, are busily preparing even now to make the next national election a competition in patrioteering with the prize of office to go to the man or the party which can prove that it has hated Russia loudest, longest, and with the most irresponsible invective.

Confidence in ourselves, confidence in mankind, the natural, normal, decent confidence of men of courage and character, has all but vanished from the Congress of the United States. And in the prolonged and inexplicable silence of the President there are few voices raised anywhere for what we used to think of as the American cause: the cause of the human future.

These two things, the affirmation of belief in the future, the surrender to fear for the future, do not go together. Above all, they do not go together in this room. If you are educating young men and young women for life, to live their lives — which is what liberal education is — you are not educating them for a vast and terrible struggle for survival to be fought between civilian populations, first with terror, and then with scientific devices for extermination.

And if, by the same sign, you believe that you are engaged in such a struggle of competitive terrorization and eventual

destruction of civilian populations, with survival, to say nothing of "victory," depending on the reactions of your people
to attack, you will not offer young men and young women
liberal education. You will offer instead the kind of education
some of our more demoralized politicians propose even now
for the production of scientists. You will produce not men
and women but Cold-War Soldiers, reared in antiseptic ignorance of every doubt or hope or aspiration, indoctrinated rather
than instructed, whose neuter and unasking minds, packed
with creed instead of questions like so many sawdust dolls,
will give to every stimulus the appropriate response. It is not
only the bigger bombs and the bigger bombers of the jingo
press we need. If we are really engaged in a civilian struggle
for survival, our greatest need is for a civilian population
disciplined for such a struggle. We need, not colleges and universities, but arsenals of human beings. And we need them
now.

These two things, the act of confidence in the future here,
the terror of the future everywhere and here as well, can
simply not be reconciled. They cannot live together. And yet
they do. They do, within this room. How do they?

Is it because people like us, people of our kind, live our
lives in separate compartments — because we don't permit
ourselves to know, as officers and teachers and students and
friends of this college, what we know only too well, what we
lie awake at night knowing, as men and women? Because we
go on with our lives and our occupations out of habit and sheer
inertia, repeating, now that they are meaningless, the forms
and motions that once had meaning when the future was alive?

Is it because we deceive ourselves with hopes which we
know only too well are deceptions — the hope that something will turn up even now, that something will happen, that

Stalin will die or the Communists will change their minds or the Titoists will overthrow the Kremlin and everything will be different: the hope that the Cold War can be won as a cold war, in spite of the fact that a cold war, by hypothesis, is a war that can never be won because it is waged, not to accomplish something, but to prevent something from happening, and is therefore only effective as long as it goes on preventing?

Is it because we delude ourselves into thinking that somehow, in some way, by some miracle, *we* will be spared in this holocaust — *our* lives will be spared, or *our* days, or *our* college or *these* particular beginnings we inaugurate this morning? Is it because we think, like the Princes in Li Po's poem, that the howling of the yellow dogs is not for us?

I, for myself, do not think so. I do not think it is for any of these reasons we are able to do what we are doing here today. I do not think we are deluding ourselves, or hiding our fears from our hopes, or carrying on out of habit, or pretending not to know what in fact we *do* know.

I think the truth is the opposite. I think the truth is that we *do not* know what we *pretend* to know — what we pretend to know because we hear ourselves saying it over and over like parrots, or because we read it over and over in the speech the hypnotized politicians are constantly making, the same speech over and over with nothing but the speaker changing.

I think we *do not* know — we here in this room and millions of others in millions of other rooms across this country — I think we *do not* know that our time is a time of ineluctable war, of inescapable struggle for survival, which weapons and warfare must decide because only weapons and warfare *can* decide it.

I think we do not know this because we know it is not true. And I think the reason we know it is not true is not that we

are childish as a people, but precisely that we are not childish.
To believe that the great crises of human history are not
resolved by threats and not resolved by arms is not childish.
To believe that the fundamental choice between individual
freedom and institutional authority which our world must
make is not a choice which bombs *can* make for us, and therefore not a choice which bombs *will* make for us, is not childish. The childish thing is the infantile mentality, the movie-
magazine mind, which thinks a crisis like the crisis of our age
can be the work of a handful of conspiratorial Communists,
and *can* be resolved, and therefore *must* be resolved, by
weapons.

We know very well we must arm ourselves for our own
defense in a world in which Russia is armed. But we do not
know, because we do not believe, that arms will be enough
no matter how many, no matter how powerful. We do not
believe this because we do not believe the decision can be
reached by arms. We do not believe that what is in issue
in our time is susceptible of armed decision.

There could be war. There could easily be war. Russian
conduct over the past three years has been provocative and
infuriating: a combination of calculated bluster and blundering deceit which only the gangster underworld could equal.
The conduct of some Americans has been stupid and provocative also. It would be hard to equal, anywhere but in Russia
itself, the irresponsibility and recklessness of certain members
of the last two Congresses and certain newspapers and certain
columnists. But because we could blunder into war with Russia through stupidity on either side, it does not follow that
war with Russia is inevitable. And it is the *inevitability* of
war which is the central question for this country, because it
is the shadow of that fatality which freezes the creative im-
pulses of our lives and exposes the most precious thing in

America — the independence and self-respect of individual citizens — to the campaigns of dishonor and defamation which have become the political stock in trade of ambitious and unprincipled politicians.

What is really in issue between the Russians and ourselves — what the evangelists of the inevitable conflict talk about day after day — is difference in belief. War is inevitable because our beliefs are different and because neither can live in a world dominated by the other. We, in the United States, must have a world in which individual liberty can thrive, for unless individual liberty can thrive throughout the world it cannot thrive here. The Russians must have a world in which authority is safe from freedom, for unless authority is safe from the aspirations of freedom everywhere it is safe from them nowhere. Therefore, the preachment goes, war must some day come, and until it comes the threat of war must be maintained.

But the evangelists of war forget two things. And it is these two things we and people like us remember, whatever words we use. They forget, first, that when they talk about the world they are not talking about the people of Russia and the United States alone. They are talking, as well, about 1400 million others who, as Secretary Acheson pointed out in his magnificent San Francisco address, are now stirring and moving in the long dream of their history as men have never stirred and moved before. Whether the world will be authoritarian or free, will depend on the 1400 million as well as on ourselves. It will depend on the world they make for themselves — the world they are even now in the process of making. For the great central fact before us, the fact to which the evangelists of war have shut their eyes, is the new world — the fact that a new and wholly different world is

in the process of creation in our time — the fact that it is
this new world, this different world, which is the ineluctable
event and for which we must prepare ourselves or perish.

That is one thing the evangelists of war forget. The other
is this: that creation is not accomplished with weapons. You
cannot make a world with weapons. You cannot shape a
world in the image of liberty with weapons. You cannot even
shape a world in the image of authority with weapons. Arms
can be used to put down freedom, as they have been used
again and again in human history. Arms can be used to overthrow authority, as we used them once, and as other peoples
have used them both before and since. But they cannot be
used to create. And the problem, both for us and for the
Russians, is to create — to create in the new world the kind
of life we severally believe in, the one kind or the other. It
is there, on *that* battlefield, on the competitive battlefield of
creative labor, not on the impotent battlefield of exterminating
war, that the real issue will be decided. It is *that* struggle
which is inescapable: *that* conflict, and not the conflict of
arms, which must be faced.

To which the realists reply: Ah, yes, but do the Russians
know it? What will the Russians be doing while we create a
world? Cutting our throats? Blasting us off the earth? No,
there's nothing the Russians understand but force: nothing
they respect but facts in being. All we can do is face them
with force and facts until — what? The voice drags off into
silence. Until they recognize the facts and say so? And
what then? Will we believe what they say? Or go on with
the force and the facts in the same old impotence until we
come to the one conclusion to which force and facts invariably
lead — the conclusion the hardheaded men have been telling
us all along we would come to — the conclusion of war?

It is one of the defects of the American educational system, and has been for generations, that it turns out a self-styled "realist" mentality which equates belief in life with gullibility, and regards a fact as a fact only when it is ugly. No one can say, of course, what the Russians think. But every indication we have — even the sadistic and brutal "trials" and the palpably engineered "confessions" — every indication we have suggests that the Russians know very well where the struggle will be decided. Why otherwise torture their victims for confessions of guilt involving their enemies? Why not shoot them offhand and be done with it? It is not for themselves or for us these grizzly dramas are played out, but for the audience of mankind.

When the Russians announced a little while ago that they were developing atomic energy for the purposes of peace — to "free mankind from its ancient servitude to toil" — the hardheaded realists in America shouted "propaganda." What the Russians were really doing, they said, was building atomic bombs — hydrogen bombs maybe — anyway bombs. Perhaps it *was* propaganda; if it was, it was good propaganda for the 1400 million — better propaganda than ours with our promise of death by incineration on a bigger and better model than Hiroshima. But perhaps also — as a writer in *The Christian Science Monitor* quietly pointed out — perhaps it wasn't propaganda after all. Perhaps the Russians really knew what they were doing. Perhaps they realized that a great new source of industrial power put at the disposal of their political philosophy might give them an advantage, previously enjoyed by us, in the struggle for men's minds. Perhaps nothing would suit them better in Russia than precisely the delusive realism of our realistic men: the concentration upon bombs and weapons while the Russians went about their business of constructing the means to wage the actual struggle — the struggle for the creation of a world.

The *Monitor* correspondent may be right. But whatever
the Russians intend or believe, the explanation of the American paradox lies in the fact that a great part of the American
people feels in its bones, whatever words it may find in its
mouth, that the conflict which divides our time is not a Rus-
sian-American conflict only, to be waged by facing up to the
Soviets with a show of defensive force, however necessary
the possession of defensive force may be. A great part of the
American people believes that the real conflict is a very different conflict, a much broader conflict — a conflict for the soul
and spirit of a world now coming into being: a new world.
It is this profound conviction which explains the national
restlessness under the negative and defensive foreign policy of
the past four years. It is this conviction which explains the
failure of the Formosa party in the Senate, even with the
support of powerful sections of the press, to make any impres-
sion whatever on the country. It is this conviction which supported the enormous and spontaneous enthusiasm aroused
by the McMahon proposals. It is this conviction which is
expressed from day to day across the country in actions like
the action in this room, actions directed toward the future
in confidence and faith.

There is a considerable body of Americans who, for all
the talk, for all *their* talk, do not believe in the inevitable war,
do not believe in the inescapable disaster, do not believe that
the destiny of the Republic is to resist history and to oppose
it, do not believe that the appearance of Communism, or the
rise of Russia, or the invention of atomic bombs, has changed
the role this people has to play. There is a considerable body
of Americans who believe that the great decisions of history
are made not by death but by life, and that we have a stake
in life, and a talent for life, and that it is there, in the shaping

of a new world, that that talent can be used and that stake protected and the decision made.

We are not, after all, a new and inexperienced people. We have governed ourselves for close to two centuries. We have seen something of human history on this planet and we have drawn our own conclusions from what we have seen. We know what it is to want what the peoples of Asia want and the peoples of Africa and Europe. We know what can happen when the great currents of life break over the banks of the old restrictions and move out toward the future. We believe, on the basis of what we have seen in this world, that men, if they can, will move toward freedom: that the desire for freedom and fulfillment is the law of the life of men as the pull of the earth is the law of the life of things. We believe, therefore, that if this new great stirring of mankind is freed of its necessities the world will move toward us. And it is there, in that labor, not in an insane and ruinous war, that we believe the struggle will be truly joined.

The paradox, then, resolves itself in that juncture. For if you believe, in spite of the squeaking ghosts, that life will go on in this earth, you prepare for life: you educate for life. Whatever your tongue may say, your heart continues to believe, and your actions are truer than your words — as this action here is truer than our words who take part in it — this action by which this college and this woman commit themselves once more to a belief in the free and creative future of mankind.

1950

13

To Make Men Free

We are not frozen into the backward-facing impotence of those societies, fixed in the rigidness of an official dogma, to which the future is the mirror of the past. We are free to make the future for ourselves.

13

TO MAKE MEN FREE

"ENGLISH," said John Keats, "ought to be kept up." He meant, by those who use it to write with. He could equally well have meant, by those who use it to govern themselves.

In a country the size of ours, faced with the problems which face us, public discourse tends to conduct itself in a currency of words like blank checks: unspecified drafts upon intellectual credit like Freedom and Democracy and Americanism. Unless the language is "kept up" by constant scrutiny and challenge, meanings will be falsified either by negligence or by such deliberate tampering as characterizes the methods of at least one notorious contemporary politician. In Russia, where such tampering is official practice, the word *democracy,* which once meant the government of the people by themselves, has been falsified to mean the government of the people by the political police.

The word freedom is in danger of the same debasement here. Freedom, in American usage, means the freedom of the individual human being to think for himself and to come to the truth by the light of his own mind and conscience. It is the freedom defined by the American Constitution. Congress is forbidden to make any law abridging the freedom of speech. There is to be no establishment of religious authority or supervision. There is to be no meddling, in other words, by state or by church with a man's thoughts or what he chooses to say about them. When it comes to thoughts, when it comes to ideas, when it comes to opinions and their expression, a man is free. His freedom is guaranteed by the fundamental law of the Republic. The opinions of others are not to be imposed upon him, no matter whose opinions they may be — the opinions of a church or the opinions of the government or the opinions of his fellow citizens — even the opinions of a majority of his fellow citizens.

A man's freedom to believe, that is to say, does not depend on *what* he believes. It does not depend on his being "right" as others see the right, no matter how numerous they may be or how well entrenched or how powerful. Right and wrong as others judge the right and wrong are irrelevant to the American conception of freedom to think and believe and say. That, of couse, is the nub of the whole matter, and the essential distinction between freedom as we mean it and freedom as it is meant in certain other quarters of the earth. In the American conception of freedom, the man and his conscience come first and the established opinions, the accepted verities, the official views come after.

Strangers to the American tradition find this aspect of our historical belief in freedom difficult, if not impossible, to accept. Their inclination is to interpret freedom to mean freedom to think *right* thoughts. Which means, freedom to think as they think, and, by enlargement, freedom to think as their friends think, or their party, or their church, or their veterans' organization, or their union, or their professional association, or whatever. The majority, the institution, the accepted opinion comes first with them and the man and his conscience nowhere. Freedom is freedom to be like everybody else, to think as the majority in the town or state or country thinks, to teach what the legislature or the dominant political or religious opinion wants taught, to conform.

The pressure which the word freedom has been under in the past few years is a pressure of this character: a pressure from those who have never really accepted or wholly understood the meaning of the word in its American use. There are some, of course, who deliberately reject the American meaning — who would destroy it if they could, replacing it with an interpretation more amenable to their own beliefs — but they are not numerous as yet. The real danger to freedom in the United States — to the word and to the thing — is the danger of the impairment of the American usage by negligence and default. Unless we can maintain the pure traditional meaning of the word — unless we can understand in common and as a nation that the only opinion established in this country by the American Constitution is the opinion that a man is free to hold *any* opinion — unless we can agree among ourselves that by freedom we mean precisely *freedom*, we may end by finding ourselves "free" in the sense in which the Russians now find themselves "democratic."

The process of debasement of the coinage has already gone some distance. Freedom in America has begun to mean not freedom itself but the majority view of freedom: the view held by most of us that freedom, under the conditions of the world we live in, is first and foremost freedom from the Communist police state. The consequence is that freedom is no longer the right of any man to hold whatever opinion he pleases. Freedom is the body of opinion opposed to the establishment of the Communist police state; and the right to hold pro-Communist opinions is, therefore, not included or protected. The recent decision of the Supreme Court in the case of the Communist leaders, and the reactions of the public and the press to that decision, make the point. Justices Black and Douglas asserted in their dissenting opinions that the effect of the decision was to make opinions and their advocacy punishable without more, and thus to restrict freedom of opinion and freedom of belief as they had not before been restricted in American history. The majority opinion admitted, though it undertook to justify, the restriction. And nevertheless the decision was applauded in the press and throughout the country as a victory for freedom.

To applaud a restriction of freedom as a victory for freedom is — whatever else may be said of it — to corrupt the word. And the case of the Communist leaders is not the only indication that just such a corruption has occurred in the common usage of the word in the United States. Not only legislative committees of the state and federal governments but vigilante groups of private citizens have undertaken, in the name of freedom, to conduct what are, in effect, raids on the essential freedoms of the citizens of the Republic. And political caucuses and conventions have applauded, as services to the cause of freedom, actions which men who understood the meaning of the word could only condemn as offensive to the fundamental concept of individual liberty.

The justification for all this, of course, is a justification with which we are only too familiar. Communism is the mortal enemy and Communism must be destroyed even at the cost of certain of our own liberties — even at the more lasting cost of the integrity of the word central to our purposes as a people. Freedom-from-Communism is now more important than freedom itself, and since we must choose between the two it is the first we must elect. The difficulty with this position is that, even if it provided a convincing justification for the acts committed under cover of its rhetoric, it would not be true. When freedom is sacrificed, freedom-from-Communism suffers also. For the most powerful defense against Communism in any country is precisely the people's realization of the distinction between Communism in action and freedom itself.

What men detest in Communism is its denial in theory, and

she 177

its destruction in practice, of the human attribute we have declared in our constitution, and asserted in our actions, we value above anything in this world: the singularity, the uniqueness, the spiritual personality of the individual human being. Men hate and detest Communism because it turns men into Members: because it suppresses and eradicates those differences and those distinctions between one man and another which we have defended as the principal worth and richness of human life: because it imposes on all men the kind of intellectual conformity, of subservience to official opinion, which we have rejected in our fundamental law and which earlier generations of Americans rejected in their lives.

To blur or to smudge this distinction between the Communist world and our own is not to injure the Communists but powerfully to assist them. And the moment we tamper with the meaning of the word freedom to make it describe conformity instead of individuality — the moment we speak of the mutilation of individual freedom as a victory for freedom — the distinction begins to disappear. The United States Senator who is applauded in freedom's name for assaults upon the individual freedom of American citizens — assaults even upon their means of livelihood and their dignity as men — is obscuring the distinction between the Communist tyranny and the democratic hope; and those who applaud him are helping to obscure it.

The Texas legislature which votes, 130 to 1, to demand the ouster from the State University of a professor who has described free enterprise as decadent, and which cuts by $6500 the salary of the University Chancellor who, supported by his Board of Regents, refuses to comply, is turning freedom in Texas into something which begins to resemble what the Communists also call freedom.

The majority of the Board of Regents of the University of

California which attempts to impose a special loyalty oath
on the University's teachers, in order to protect the freedom
of American instiutions, is bringing American institutions
that much closer to those very different institutions which special oaths and special penalties protect — the institutions of
the totalitarian world: Stalin's and Franco's and Perón's and
Mao's.

The California Court which passed on the constitutionality
of the Regents' action had the courage to say as much: "While
the Court is mindful of the fact that the action of the Regents
was, at the outset, motivated by a desire to protect the University from the influence of subversive elements dedicated to
the overthrow of our constitutional government . . . we are
also keenly aware that, equal to the danger of subversion
from without by means of force and violence, is the danger
of subversion from within by the gradual whittling away and
disintegration of the very pillars of our freedom."

The Court's language is worth pondering. Why "subversion from within by the gradual whittling away . . . of the
very pillars of our freedom"? What "freedom" was being
whittled away by the action of the Board of Regents of the
University of California? The freedom of those to whom their
action applied: the University's teachers. But what freedom
of the University's teachers was affected? The freedom to
think for themselves without the meddling of the state or its
authorities. But why is the freedom to think for oneself — the
mere freedom of a teacher to think for himself — why is this
freedom a "pillar" of the great freedom which is the Republic?
Because the freedom of the mind is the freedom of the man
and the freedom of the man is what the Republic *is*.

But why is the whittling away of this freedom of the mind,
of the man, "subversive"? Why is it "subversive" even though

it is undertaken in the name of the defense of the United States *against* subversion? Because it is this freedom of the mind, of the man, which is the rock on which the United States is founded. To diminish it is to diminish the country. Even though it is diminished in the country's name. Even though those who diminish it declare their opinion that, without some limitation upon the freedom of the mind, the freedom of the man, the country will be lost.

The Court's reasoning is plain enough. The moment you allow a government's conviction, or an institution's conviction, or a majority's conviction of its own rightness to justify its power to silence those who disagree with it, just at that moment you surrender the fundamental American Proposition, and the moment you surrender the American Proposition your surrender the Republic. There is no stopping place beyond: no halfway mark. It makes no difference whether the conviction of self-rightness is religious, as it was with the majority in Massachusetts Bay three hundred years ago and has been since with majorities made up of other sects, Protestant as well as Catholic; or whether the conviction is economic, as it is now with the believers in economic determinism and was once with the believers in laissez-faire; or whether the conviction is political or racial or social or whatever it is. Once you permit those who are convinced of their own superior rightness to censor and restrict the opinions of others, you open the gate to the silencing and the suppression of the opinions of others, and once you permit the silencing and the suppression of opinions because governments or institutions or majorities don't like them, just at that moment the citadel has been surrendered. For the American citadel is *a man*. Not man in general. Not man in the abstract. Not the majority of men. But man. *That* man. *His* worth. *His* uniqueness.

His quality in himself. That in him which is uniquely his and which enriches, therefore, the world.

You cannot defend that citadel, and you cannot defend this country, by ambiguity either of word or action. Above all you cannot defend them by giving freedom a double meaning — by saying that freedom in the country has won a great victory when freedom in the man has suffered a mortal wound. Freedom in American usage means freedom *of* the man, and freedom of the man means freedom of the man's mind. The man comes first and everything else comes after — the establishments of opinion — the official views. The American Proposition refers not, as the editors of *Fortune* magazine have recently suggested, to American industry, but to the American people. It is an American Proposition as to man's place in the universe, not as to the production of durable goods. And what it advances is the worth of man, the worth of the human individual — not the superiority of a given economic or religious or political system.

The American Proposition is the proposition, advanced at the beginnings of the Republic and enacted into law when the Constitution was adopted, that a man's freedom to be a man, and to find and speak the truth that is in him, is more important than the protection of any accepted belief, and official verity, against criticism, against challenge, against dissent. More important not only to that man but to all men, to the society which all men compose, to the nation, to the world, to life itself. It is a proposition, in other words, which rests upon an act of faith, the most courageous of all earthly acts of faith — an act of faith in man and in the God whom man, in the freedom of his conscience and his thought, can find.

When it was first enacted into law the American Proposition was new. It is still new: the one wholly new and revolutionary idea the modern world has produced, for all its triumphs in science and technique — an idea so new and so revolutionary in its literal and explicit meaning that half the patriotic societies which celebrate their attachment to the American Revolution have yet to understand it or accept it. But it is new and revolutionary, not solely because it proclaims human liberty, nor solely because it founds its conception of human liberty on the freedom of the individual human mind, defending that freedom in the most explicit and peremptory terms against the tyranny of organized opinion. It is new and revolutionary because of the act of faith which it expresses.

Our reliance in this country is on the inquiring, individual human mind. Our strength is founded there: our resilience, our ability to face an ever changing future and to master it. We are not frozen into the backward-facing impotence of those societies, fixed in the rigidness of an official dogma, to which the future is the mirror of the past. We are free to make the future for ourselves. And we are free because it is the man who counts in this country: always and at every moment and in any situation, the man. Not the Truth but the man: not the truth as the state sees the truth or as the church sees the truth or as the majority sees the truth or as the mob sees the truth, but the truth as the man sees it, as the man finds it, for himself as man. Our faith is in the infinite variety of human beings and in the God who made them various and of many minds; in their singularity, their uniqueness, the creativeness of the differences between them. Our faith, in simple, sober truth, is in the human Being, the human spirit, the hungers and the longings that lead it toward its images of truth, its perceptions of the beauty of the world.

Those who launched the great human adventure which this Republic is, dared to put their trust in the individual man, the man alone, the man thinking for himself. They dared to believe in a *people,* which is a nation of individual men constituting among themselves a society; for a people is not what the totalitarians call "the masses"; a people is an agreement of many alone to make together a world in which each one of them can live as himself. The founders of the American Republic believed in a people. They not only provided no censors for the thoughts of those who were to come after them: they prohibited censors. They not only provided no moral or intellectual or religious authority to govern the beliefs of their successors: they rejected forever the establishment of any such authority. They trusted men.

It is in that trust that the Republic can still be defended. Indeed it is only in that trust that it can be defended as the kind of country it is. To attempt to defend it otherwise — to attempt, above all, to defend it by debasing the coinage of meaning in which its nature is expressed — is to lose both the country itself and the struggle against Communism which is cited as justification of the fraud. If freedom can come to mean something less than freedom in the general mind, it can come to mean the opposite of freedom. If freedom ceases to express the American faith in man and in man's unqualified right to find the truth for himself, it will shortly express a faith in established truth, in the rightness of official opinion. When that happens we shall have lost both the American Proposition and the fight against Communism. For the one idea that can triumph over the police-state notion that the truth is already known, once for all, and that the truth is therefore entitled to impose itself by force, is the American Proposition that a man is free to find the truth for himself. It is the one idea that can triumph because, as long as it is held, man himself is the cause of those who hold it. And against that cause no enemy has prevailed for long.

1951

Acknowledgments

All but three chapters in this volume are based on articles that originally appeared in the following magazines, the editors of which have kindly granted permission for their inclusion here:

"Thirteen Candles: One for Every State." *Life*, May 31, 1948 (under the title "Last Soldiers of the Revolution").

"The Unimagined America." *The Atlantic Monthly*, June 1943.

"Notes on the Image of Man in These Mornings." *Poetry*, October-November 1948.

"The Conquest of America." *The Atlantic Monthly*, August 1949.

"The Revulsion of Decency." *The American Scholar*, Fall 1950.

"The Sense of American Purpose." *ADA World*, February 1951 (under the title "The Dialectic of Freedom").

"The Power of Choice." *The Atlantic Monthly*, August 1951.

"The Belief in Man." *The Atlantic Monthly*, November 1944.

"The Act of Faith." *The Atlantic Monthly*, June 1950.

"To Make Men Free." *The Atlantic Monthly*, November 1951.

Index